HOCKEY'S HOTTEST PLAYERS

The On- & Off-Ice Stories of the Superstars

Arpon Basu

OVER TIME BOOKS

The Publisher: OverTime Books is an imprint of Éditions de
             la Montagne Verte

Library and Archives Canada Cataloguing in Publication

Basu, Arpon, 1976–
   Hockey's hottest players : the on- and off-ice stories of
   the superstars / Arpon Basu.

   ISBN-13: 978-0-9737681-3-8
   ISBN-10: 0-9737681-3-4

 1. Hockey players—Biography. 2. National Hockey League—
Biography. I. Title.

GV848.5.A1B38   2005 796.962'092'2   C2005-905013-6

Project Director: Jay Poulton
Project Editor: Kathy van Denderen
Production: Jodene
Cover Design: Valentino
Cover Image: Jarome Iginla. Courtesy of Getty Images / Dave
Sandford (photographer).

PC: P5

Contents

Dedication

To my mother, Nila, and father, Dipak, who made great sacrifices so that I may grow up in the land where hockey is king.

Introduction

The National Hockey League (NHL) is emerging from the darkest period of its long and storied history. Although league commissioner Gary Bettman wanted desperately for the NHL to be first in the hearts and minds of the entire continent's sports fans, becoming the first North American major sports league to lose an entire season to a labour dispute was not really what he had in mind.

So how will the NHL, and by extension the game of hockey, emerge from the year-long lockout to convince fans to spend their hard-earned dollars on a sport that has essentially given them all a collective slap in the face? It will attempt to do so by improving its on-ice product, giving a game that was bogged down by overly defensive strategies a new life with various rule changes meant to increase offence and excitement for the fans who are the league's lifeline.

But the NHL will also need some star power to put people back in the seats. Since Wayne Gretzky's retirement, the league has not had a single player on which it could hang its hat. Mario Lemieux came back after retiring with back problems and other ailments, but he is not the same player he once was, and his injury concerns make him an unsuitable candidate to be the NHL's post-lockout poster boy.

The new and improved NHL will need a player who is just hitting his prime, someone who can promote the league both to fans and corporations for years to come, someone who can transcend the game like Gretzky once did. If such a person exists, he may come from the group of 12 players profiled in this book. None of them were 30 years old when the 2005–06 NHL season began, and they are all stars.

Of course, there are many other players who also could have been included in this book, such as Boston Bruins centre Joe Thornton, Minnesota Wild sniper Marian Gaborik and Philadelphia Flyers winger Simon Gagné, to name a few.

But the ones selected here are the crème de la crème, the elite young NHL players who have the most potential to carry the league's fortunes into this new era of professional hockey, one that the NHL hopes will be its most prosperous ever.

Only time will tell if they are successful, but for the fans, watching them try will be a lot of fun.

Chapter One

Rick Nash

R ick Nash would have gladly waited his turn. Sitting at the 2002 NHL entry draft in the home arena of his beloved Toronto Maple Leafs, surrounded by 50 of his family and friends who made the short drive from his hometown of Brampton, Ontario, Nash thought he had it all figured out. He'd read the scouting lists and hockey pundits who said smooth-skating Medicine Hat Tigers defenceman Jay Bouwmeester was a lock to go to the Florida Panthers with the first pick, and he believed them. Why wouldn't he? He was, after all, only six days from his 18th birthday, barely even an adult. Who was he to question the experts?

But what Nash forgot while getting swept up in the pomp and pageantry of the biggest day of his hockey life was the interview he had with Columbus Blue Jackets general manager Doug MacLean, who held the third pick in the draft. "I'd love to have you," MacLean told Nash, "but I don't know if I'm going to get you at number three."

Nash, obviously flattered by MacLean's desire to have him on his team, paused a moment before coming up with what he felt was a perfectly reasonable solution to MacLean's dilemma. "Well," Nash said, "why don't you go get me."

Sitting in the stands of the Air Canada Centre at the draft a few days later, Nash didn't believe for a second that MacLean would take his brazen advice so seriously. But Nash's response had only confirmed what MacLean already knew—he'd do whatever it took to get Nash into a Blue Jackets uniform.

Panthers general manager Rick Dudley had openly coveted Bouwmeester but started wavering in the weeks leading up to the draft, enough to cause concern in Columbus. MacLean knew that Atlanta Thrashers general manager Don Waddell had essentially decided he needed a franchise goaltender and would take Finland's Kari Lehtonen. If Dudley was being more open about favouring Bouwmeester, MacLean could have sat back and waited for Nash to fall down to him. But with Dudley flirting with the idea of grabbing Nash, MacLean had to move.

Minutes before Dudley was to make his first pick, MacLean offered him the Blue Jackets pick at number three and the option to swap picks with

Columbus in 2003. Dudley snapped up the deal after sending Waddell a couple of late-round picks to ensure he didn't select Bouwmeester, and MacLean had his prize. While all this wheeling and dealing was transpiring, Nash was still thinking about all those scouting lists he'd read over the past weeks and months. "I was sitting there just thinking about Bouwmeester going first to Florida and the next thing you hear there's been a trade," Nash said. "My stomach just dropped...it was like going on a big roller coaster."

After consummating the most important trade in Columbus franchise history, MacLean walked to the podium and announced that Rick Nash was the number one pick in the 2002 NHL entry draft. The Nash clan, all 50 of them, went crazy with joy. All except for one.

"Everybody said he'd probably go third before the draft," recalled Nash's mother, Liz. "After he was picked number one, I didn't even cry because I was in such shock."

For MacLean, he saw his bold draft-day manoeuvring as a necessity if he wanted to get any sleep that night. "I haven't said it very often," MacLean said later, "but I would have been sick to my stomach leaving the draft without him."

Although Nash wasn't aware of it that day, he was on the road to superstardom, a road that began on a tiny pond in Brampton. Nash's father, Jamie, and older brother, James, first got Nash into a pair of skates when he was only two years old, having barely learned how to walk.

"He was a good skater," Liz Nash said. "He was skating backwards before most of the other kids were skating forwards."

Nash has been on the fast track ever since. He dominated the Greater Toronto minor hockey ranks, and when a growth spurt hit at age 14, Nash's reputation grew as well. By the time he made it to his bantam draft year with the Toronto Marlboros in 1999, he was one of the top forwards in Ontario, if not in Canada. He scored a staggering 61 goals with 54 assists for 115 points in only 34 games that year, showing off his soft hands, long reach and deceptive speed for a gangly kid. But most of all, Nash displayed a wonderful sense of timing.

Dale Hunter, the 19-year NHL veteran and the owner, general manager and coach of the Ontario Hockey League's (OHL) London Knights, went to a prospects tournament to get a look at Nash in person to prepare for the bantam draft.

"He had two goals in the first five minutes we saw him" Hunter recalled. "But at the end of the game he had an empty-net breakaway [for a hat trick], and he unselfishly passed the puck." Hunter didn't need to think long to decide who he would take with the fourth pick in the 2000 bantam draft.

Nash continued the success he had known his whole hockey-playing life in London, posting 31 goals and 35 assists in 58 games in 2000–01 to finish second on the team in points and first in goals. That performance easily earned him the OHL's rookie of the year award, and he was placed on the Canadian Hockey League's first all-rookie team.

Nash also made his international debut that year, winning a bronze medal with Team Ontario at the 2001 Under-17 World Hockey Challenge in Nova Scotia. He finished second on the team in scoring with 5 goals and 2 assists in four games, and in one game he scored 2 goals in only 11 seconds. Detroit Red Wings scout Joe McDonnell was one of the roughly 10 scouts from various levels that watched Nash play in the tournament, and he was impressed with the teenager's skill set.

"He's a total package," McDonnell said. "Size, skill, hockey sense—whatever you look for in a player, he's got it all."

In August 2001, Nash won a gold medal with the Canadian under-18 team at the Six Nations Cup, leading the team in scoring with 5 goals and 5 assists in five games, including a hat trick and 2 assists in Canada's 9–4 win over Russia in the gold medal game. That set Nash up for his NHL draft year with the Knights, where he once again excelled with a team-high 32 goals and 40 assists playing on a lower-rung team.

Nash was also a source of comic relief in the dressing room, keeping the team loose, even when things weren't going so well on the ice. A favourite pastime of Nash and his teammates was going out to the local mall in London, gluing loonies to the floor and then laughing at the people trying to pick them up. One of his fellow Knights, Logan Hunter (the coach's nephew), remembers another one of Nash's favourite pranks.

"Rick does a pretty good impression of our assistant coach, Jacques Beaulieu, so right at the trade deadline, he was calling kids and telling them they'd been traded," Hunter recalled with a laugh. "Had some of them going pretty good."

Despite his great performances on and off the ice, what really set Nash apart and caught the eye of every NHL scout was his selection for the 2002 Canadian world junior team as a 17-year-old, making him the youngest player on the team. Barry Trapp, the Toronto Maple Leafs director of amateur scouting, Hockey Canada's director of scouting at the time, remembers giving Nash two strikes before he even stepped on the ice.

"At the world juniors, I made it clear I didn't want any 17-year-olds," Trapp said. "But anywhere we put him—at centre, right or left wing—he'd score a goal. He made us take him."

Nash began as a third or fourth liner on head coach Stan Butler's team but eventually worked his way to a regular shift, scoring a goal and adding an assist as Canada played Russia in the final to take the silver medal in the tournament held in the Czech Republic. His performance left a lasting impression on Butler. "I've never seen a player step in at such a young age and be able to dominate a game the way he has," Butler said. "He's a great player."

When Nash returned to the lowly Knights after playing with the best teenagers on the planet, he practically took on the OHL by himself. His Knights limped into the playoffs with the eighth and final seed, giving them a date with the league's best regular season squad in 2001–02, the Plymouth Whalers.

But Nash was a man possessed over the six game series. He led London to a 4–2 series upset with 6 goals and 4 assists. The superhuman performance made him a lock to be one of the first names called at the NHL draft later on that summer.

"He really matured in the postseason," Detroit Red Wings assistant general manager Jim Nill said in the weeks preceding the draft. "He became a leader. Everybody knows his skill level—he has a good feel for the ice, he sees the goal and the seams so well— but put that together with his leadership, and that's why he's going to be a top pick."

It was words like these that made the Blue Jackets MacLean so nervous at the draft, forcing him to swing the deal that had changed Nash's life forever. All of a sudden, the 18-year-old was no longer just a great hockey prospect, he was a number one NHL draft pick, one that led his team to mortgage the following year's draft to have a chance at landing him.

"I sure hope [MacLean] thinks he made the right choice," Nash said later. "He showed a lot of confidence in switching the draft picks and that put a lot of pressure on me to perform."

So Nash performed, and he didn't waste much time, either. In his first NHL game, suiting up as the youngest player in the NHL, he scored the game-tying goal in a 2–1 comeback win over the Chicago Blackhawks on October 10, 2002, making him only the eighth number one draft pick in NHL history to score a goal in his first game.

Although he said before the season began that he only wanted to stay in Columbus the whole year, Nash finished that rookie season with 17 goals and 22 assists in 74 games, coming second in the Calder Trophy balloting for NHL rookie of the year and taking part in the YoungStars Game during all-star weekend.

Nash grew up a lot that rookie year as well. He refused the Blue Jackets' offer to set him up with a billet family in favour of getting his own place. Most NHL teams don't allow an 18-year-old kid—especially one they had just signed for over $8.5 million—to live on his own in a strange town, but Columbus was confident that Nash was mature enough to handle it.

"Age is just a number," Nash said. "I didn't act like an 18-year-old and I couldn't be like a real 18-year-old, so why should I live like one?"

Nash, at 19, was still the youngest player in the NHL in 2003–04, but he definitely didn't play like it. He felt satisfied with his rookie year but was convinced he could have produced even more if he had some more muscle to fight off checks in front of the net. He played his rookie year at 6-foot-4 and 188 pounds, but by the time he came back to training camp in September, Nash weighed a solid 208 pounds. He put the 20 pounds of extra muscle to work immediately, going to the net harder and staying there longer. He scored 8 goals in his first 10 games and 15 in his first 23 games.

On December 6, 2003, Nash capped a five-game goal-scoring streak with his 18th of the season, surpassing the total for his entire rookie season in only his 26th game of the year. MacLean watched the spectacle with a certain degree of awe. "He's probably way ahead of where we expected him to be when we drafted him. When you draft an 18-year-old, you're always a little nervous," MacLean said in October of that year. "Our people felt he was going to be a star in the league but, I mean, he's on pace for 50 goals right now."

By late January 2004, Nash was the league's leading goal scorer and had scored 30.1 percent of the Blue Jackets' total, but the teenager didn't see carrying the fortunes of the entire franchise as anything to lose much sleep over. "I really don't feel too much pressure, and the club doesn't put too much pressure on me," Nash said. "I just know I am supposed to go out there and score every night."

He went back to all-star weekend that year, except this time he was suiting up in the main event. He became the youngest player to appear in an all-star game since Wendell Clark of the Toronto Maple Leafs in 1986. Nash's consistent pace contin-ued in the second half of the season, but Atlanta Thrashers winger Ilya Kovalchuk and Calgary Flames captain Jarome Iginla poured it on after the all-star break, and the three young stars tied for the league lead in goals with 41 apiece.

With that, Nash became the youngest player to win the league goal-scoring crown—a year and a half younger than Wayne Gretzky was when he won it for the 1981–82 season. Nash also became the first teenager to score 40 in a season since Jimmy Carson in 1988, and Nash's 58 career goals before the age of 20 ranks eighth in NHL history.

His breakout performance should have granted Nash superstar status, but he still wasn't recognized as one of Canada's best players, let alone the NHL's. Nash was invited to play for Canada at the senior world championships after the 2003–04 regular season was over, but he was struck with a severe case of tonsillitis the day before his departure and had to undergo surgery.

When it came time to select Canada's entry in the World Cup of Hockey, Nash's name was mentioned as a possibility. He was, after all, the NHL's leading goal scorer. But when push came to shove, Nash was deemed expendable. "Obviously it was disappointing; I thought I had a chance," Nash said later. "But they took the best players in Canada, and if I was too young or my resume didn't fit their team, then I have many years to play."

Nash did not play in the NHL in the fall of 2004 due to the lockout that cost the league an entire season. Instead, he packed his bags for Davos, Switzerland, to join the Swiss Elite League, playing on a line with Boston Bruins star Joe Thornton. While Thornton led the team with 54 points in 44 games, Nash was a close second with 46, including 26 goals. Nash scored nine times in the playoffs to help lead Davos to the Swiss championship. Although few 20-year-olds have the option of moving to Switzerland to work, the excitement of the new cultural experience seemed to wear off for the young Nash.

"Well, there's not much to do in a little town of 17,000 people," said Nash. "No movie theatre, no mall, so there wasn't much to do other than stay at the rink and hang out with the guys, go eat dinner. But it was good, it was a real laid-back environment."

Shortly after his Swiss league season came to an end, Nash was summoned once again to play for Canada at the world championships after many big-name players like Mario Lemieux, Joe Sakic and Jarome Iginla declined invitations. The world championships turned out to be Nash's international coming-out party, with hockey-starved fans worldwide watching as the NHL lockout continued.

Nash was placed back on a line with his Davos teammate Thornton and Philadelphia Flyers forward Simon Gagné on the other wing. The line was easily the best of the tournament, with Thornton finishing first in scoring with 16 points in nine games and Nash finishing a close second with 15 points, including a tournament-leading 9 goals. That earned him a spot on the tournament all-star team as Canada won the silver medal.

But one goal in particular put the spotlight squarely on Nash as the NHL's next great scoring star. In Canada's third game of the tournament, a 3–1 win over the United States, Nash streaked down the ice on a partial breakaway with U.S. defenceman Aaron Miller in hot pursuit. Keeping Miller away from the puck with his body, Nash cut across the front of the net, waited for U.S. goaltender Rick DiPietro to commit, then coolly flipped the puck over the falling DiPietro and just under the crossbar. The Canadian bench was in a state of shock.

"If you'd have seen our bench when he scored that goal," Nash's Canadian teammate Shane Doan said. "Guys were looking at each other going, 'Oh man.' He led the whole NHL in goals—I think it was the first time a teenager led the NHL in scoring since Wayne Gretzky—and you didn't really hear that much about him. It was the funniest thing. It was so quiet it was ridiculous. The league should have...I mean, the kid's incredible. And not only a great hockey player, he's the nicest guy. So respectful. And the scary thing is that he's going to get bigger. He's going to fill out more, and he's going to get stronger. He already takes the puck to the net better than anyone else in the league. He's really remarkable, he really is."

Doan has no more reason to be concerned because Nash, before even being allowed to legally drink a beer after a home game in Columbus, became a bona fide NHL superstar at the world championships. And the best is yet to come.

Just Call Me Cash

Rick Nash didn't expect to be the first player selected in the 2002 NHL entry draft. But once he was, he wasn't about to let a golden opportunity pass him by. It took Nash and Columbus Blue Jackets general manager Doug MacLean some time before coming together on a contract for the new franchise player. The negotiations began in the summer of 2002 and continued through the Blue Jackets' training camp in Summerside, Prince Edward Island.

When Nash finally signed on the dotted line, mere days before he scored his first NHL goal in his first game, he agreed to a very personalized bonus package. On top of the base annual salary of $1.185 million (rookie salaries were capped at $1.2 million at the time), Nash received a bonus package worth $8.561 million over three years. Why the extra $61,000? It matched Nash's number 61 on the back of his jersey. From that point on, his new Columbus teammates took to calling the blue-chipper "Rick Cash."

Chapter Two

Sidney Crosby

W hen the phone rang, Sidney Crosby thought
it was just another reporter calling for yet
another interview. After all, the hockey prodigy
had already handled hundreds of media interviews
before he was even old enough to drive, and this
one was probably no different. Crosby was in Los
Angeles, California, at the time, training in prepa-
ration to be the youngest player—at only 15 years
of age—to take part in Canada's under-18 national
team training camp in Calgary a few days later.

Crosby answered the phone, and the voice on the
other end of the line belonged to Donna Spencer,
a reporter for The Canadian Press wire service, and
she had some extraordinary news. A few days earlier, Wayne Gretzky—yes, The Great One—had
given what he probably thought was an innocuous
interview to a reporter with the *Arizona Republic*
newspaper in Phoenix. When the reporter asked

Gretzky if there was anyone he thought could break some of the 61 NHL scoring records he either holds or shares, he didn't expect Gretzky to mention a specific name. But, surprisingly, Gretzky did.

"Yes, Sidney Crosby, he's dynamite," Gretzky responded. "He's the best player I've seen since Mario [Lemieux]...He's that good. I went to watch him play this year, and I actually got on the ice with him. He's got it all."

Upon hearing the news of Gretzky's anointment over the phone, Crosby couldn't utter a word in response. He was numb. Finally, after gathering his thoughts, the prodigy replied to Spencer. "Wow, I hadn't heard that. That's something else. That's pretty special for Wayne Gretzky to say that. I don't think his records will ever be broken. That's a compliment for him to say that for sure."

The young man, who hadn't even taken part in a major junior hockey game or in any international competition, didn't realize it at the time, but Gretzky's compliment was the official launch party for the hockey world's brand new travelling act: The Sidney Crosby Show. It was a hit with fans desperate for a dominant offensive superstar, and Crosby suddenly became a saviour for hockey at a time when it needed one the most.

Crosby had an agent by the time he was 14, was profiled in *Sports Illustrated*, became only the fifth player to be selected to Canada's junior national team at the age of 16 and signed a multi-million dollar endorsement deal at 17. All before suiting up in a single NHL game.

Crosby's story begins much earlier, in a dingy basement in the Halifax hamlet of Cole Harbour, Nova Scotia. Crosby's father, Troy, was a goaltender in the Québec Major Junior Hockey League (QMJHL) who was drafted in the 12th round of the 1984 draft by the Montréal Canadiens. Unfortunately for Troy, the Habs had selected another goalie in the third round of that very same draft, a chap by the name of Patrick Roy, and the elder Crosby never managed to make the jump to the NHL.

Troy and Trina Crosby's first child was born August 7, 1987, the reason Crosby wears number 87 today (8th month, 7th day, '87). Before he was even three years old, his parents put young Sidney in a pair of skates. Troy helped nurture his son's love of the game by converting their basement into a mini hockey rink and would regularly don his old goalie pads so that his son could shoot at him. But Troy was forced to stop when Sidney was only nine years old because the slap shots coming at him were leaving him battered and bruised.

"He was killing me," Troy said. "I told him, 'You don't need a goalie, just shoot at the net.'"

Crosby began playing minor hockey when he was only four years old, and by the time he was

seven, he already had the first of what would soon
be hundreds of newspaper interviews under his
belt. While playing atom hockey at the age of 10,
Crosby gave an idea of how good he would become
by scoring a ridiculous 159 goals and 121 assists for
280 points in 55 games.

But when a youngster stands out that much,
especially a youngster playing hockey in Canada,
problems tend to follow. Crosby was the target of
such nasty taunts and abuse from other hockey parents that he sometimes went home from the rink
with tears streaming down his face. Troy admits that
some of the abuse directed at his son was because of
his own antics at the rink, but most of the taunts
were fuelled by petty anger, pure and simple.

One time, as an eight-year-old, Crosby was playing in a provincial playoff game. As he celebrated
one of the five goals he would score in that game,
a parent leaned over the glass and yelled at Crosby,
"Go home Crosby, you bum! You've got no skill!"

Another time, Crosby cried after a woman
called him a "prima donna" in the arena lobby. It
got so bad that Crosby took to skating in the pre-
game warm-up without his jersey so he couldn't
be identified.

"I don't know if jealousy is the right word, but
there was definitely some resentment," Trina
Crosby said. "Maybe not with the kids, but the parents. At one point, it was really hard to go to the

rink if there had been a big article about Sidney in the newspaper."

Unfortunately for Crosby, his performance on the ice made the articles, and the negative attention that resulted from them, inevitable. But he never let the verbal jabs affect his game.

"He ignores it; he walks away from it," Troy Crosby said. "I've seen people with kids of their own hanging over the glass screaming and yelling things at him, unbelievable things, when he was just nine years old. But he doesn't lower himself to their level. He just worries about Sidney and playing hockey...Wayne Gretzky, Mario Lemieux, Eric Lindros, all those people had the same problems growing up. We just move forward."

Crosby's wild success in the minor hockey ranks made him the exception to almost every age-requirement rule in Nova Scotia. At 13 years old, still PeeWee age, he made the Dartmouth Subways midget AAA team—two age groups higher than his own. Even though there was no specific rule barring a PeeWee age player from playing midget hockey, the provincial hockey council ruled he was too young, which led Crosby's father to appeal the council's decision to the higher-ranking Nova Scotia Hockey Association. While the association weighed the decision, Crosby stayed off the ice for six weeks, making him probably the youngest hockey player ever to hold out.

The appeal, however, failed, and Crosby was sent to the Cole Harbour bantam AAA Wings.

"I would have been challenged in midget," Crosby said at the time. "I'm still going to get better, but I think I would have improved a lot more in midget."

Crosby proceeded to score 86 goals with 96 assists for 182 points with the Wings, winning the 2000–01 provincial championship tournament scoring title and Most Valuable Player (MVP) award. In the summer of 2001, he was drafted with the fifth pick of the second round by the Truro Bearcats—a team in the Maritime Junior A Hockey League—just two months before his 14th birthday. The Truro general manager at the time, Steve Crowell, couldn't resist taking a flier on the phenom, even though Crosby would be putting his slight 5-foot-7, 145-pound frame on the same ice as men who were up to 21 years of age.

"They don't come along very often this skilled, this young," Crowell said after the draft. "He's got the ability to play at our level. Obviously with his size, we'll have to have lots of protection for him."

Crosby didn't sound the least bit intimidated after hearing the news. "Yeah, I can adapt to it," he said, only after noting what a surprise it was to be drafted by a junior team at age 13. "I've been adapting to each level I've gone to each year. It's no different. It's a bigger step, but I think I can do it."

He was well on his way, sitting second on Truro's training camp scoring list, when the Crosby family decided that the two-hour round-trip commute from Cole Harbour to Truro four or five times a week was too much for a ninth-grader to bear. So Crosby went back to the midget AAA Dartmouth Subways and lit it up, scoring a staggering 106 goals with 111 assists in 81 league and tournament games. He was named MVP of the 2002 provincial and Canadian championships, leading the Subways to the national final with 24 points in seven games.

Then, during that summer in Los Angeles the fateful moment came: The Next One met The Great One. Gretzky and Crosby skated on a line together in a 3-on-3 drill, and that was all it took to convince the greatest hockey player ever that he had just seen his successor.

From that point on, it seemed as if some of Gretzky's magic had rubbed off on Crosby because his stock as a household name in the world of hockey began to skyrocket. Crosby's decision in the summer of 2002 to attend Minnesota prep school Shattuck-St. Mary's instead of playing his second year of midget or Junior A hockey made for banner headlines across Atlantic Canada.

The general manager of the Halifax Mooseheads, a team in the QMJHL, tried in vain to convince the league's other teams to allow Crosby into the league as a 15-year-old player on the condition he play for his hometown team—in this case the Mooseheads. The suggestion was voted down by 11 of the league's 16 teams.

Crosby went to Minnesota partly because Shattuck-St Mary's is widely recognized as one of the best hockey training institutions in North America, but it was also to get away from the heckling and scrutiny that came with being the best young hockey player in Canada.

After scoring 72 goals with 90 assists in 57 games and leading Shattuck to the United States national midget championship, Crosby decided to enter the QMJHL draft rather than wait a year and accept one of the hundreds of college scholarship offers he'd already received. For making that choice, he was publicly thanked by the Canadian junior hockey central scouting director, probably because it made naming the top prospect for the 2005 NHL draft a cinch. The first pick that year belonged to the Rimouski Océanic, and there was no question as to who they would select.

"Rimouski did their part," Crosby said on draft day, "now I think it's time to do mine."

He didn't waste any time.

In a pre-season game, Crosby racked up 8 points, leading his teammates to start calling him Darryl, after former Maple Leafs great Darryl Sittler, who once had an NHL record 10 points in one game. In his regular season debut Crosby dazzled the crowd in Rouyn-Noranda by scoring a third period natural hat trick that included the winning goal, leading Rimouski back from a 3–0 deficit to win 4–3.

In his home debut at the Colisée de Rimouski a few nights later, Crosby scored twice—including the winner in overtime—and added 3 assists in a 7–6 win over Moncton. If there had been any doubt about Crosby's status as a hockey prodigy, he successfully erased them in just over 120 minutes of hockey.

But later in the 2003–04 season, Crosby showed off one of his greatest talents, taking some of the best elements from other players and adding them to his own repertoire. He remembered watching a goal scored by University of Michigan centre Mike Legg during the 1996 National Collegiate Athletic Association (NCAA) tournament. In that game, Legg was behind his opponents' net, left alone by the two defencemen. So he decided to lay his stick flat on the ice against the puck, swing the puck up onto the blade of his stick and tuck it into the top corner of the net lacrosse-style over the shoulder of the unsuspecting goalie. That goal tied the national quarterfinal game 2–2 as Michigan went on to win the game 4–3, and eventually the championship.

Crosby tried the same move in November in a game the Océanic was already leading 5–0 over the Québec City Remparts. With Rimouski on a power play and having been left to his own devices behind the net, Crosby executed the copy-cat play to perfection before proceeding to skate full-tilt down the ice, waving his arms in celebration. That move earned Crosby the wrath of *Hockey Night in Canada*'s Don Cherry, who on national television called the phenom a "hot dog" and warned him that if he continued behaving this way someone would hurt him in retaliation. Two days later, Cherry was summoned to address the issue at a press conference in Halifax.

"It was like I'd said something about the Pope," Cherry said on the following week's broadcast. "It was unbelievable."

Just before Christmas in 2003, Crosby fulfilled a lifelong dream when he was named to the Canadian junior national team, joining Gretzky, Eric Lindros, Jason Spezza and Jay Bouwmeester as the only players ever selected as 16-year-olds. As soon as Crosby got the news, all he could think to do was look for a phone to tell his parents.

"It felt good to make that call," Crosby said afterwards. "They've made a lot of sacrifices for me to play hockey."

Although Crosby didn't dominate the tournament, he was no slouch either, picking up 5 points in six games and becoming the youngest Canadian to score a goal in the world juniors. Crosby went back to Rimouski with a disappointing silver medal after a tough 4–3 loss to the United States in the final, but he finished his rookie year of major junior hockey strong. His 54 goals and 81 assists in 59 games not only led the QMJHL in scoring that year, it was the highest point total in the entire Canadian Hockey League (CHL). For his efforts, Crosby was named national player of the year, a feat unheard of for a rookie who was not yet draft eligible.

Crosby got off to a sluggish start—by his lofty standards—in his second season with Rimouski. He had only 74 points in his first 35 games before joining Team Canada once again for the 2005 world junior championships. Crosby's performance at the world juniors this time around, however, was far more dominant than his first. His line with Boston Bruins product Patrice Bergeron and Corey Perry of the London Knights was the dominant trio of the tournament. Crosby registered 6 goals and 3 assists in six games to help a well-balanced Canadian team win its first world junior title in eight years.

When he returned to Rimouski, Crosby moved to a new level of greatness, even for him. In his 27 regular season games as a world junior gold medallist, he compiled unthinkable numbers of 40 goals and 54 assists for 94 points, an average of nearly 3.5 points per game. His performance in the second half of the 2004–05 season gave him 66 goals and 102 assists in 62 regular season games, meaning he either got a goal or an assist on more than half of Rimouski's league-high 333 goals scored that year.

By this point in his young life, Crosby's income from endorsements was already in six figures according to his agent Pat Brisson. But in March 2005, with his popularity in Canada higher than it had ever been thanks to the world junior gold medal, he signed a five-year endorsement deal with Reebok worth a reported $2.5 million.

Crosby led Rimouski to the 2004–05 QMJHL title to earn a berth in his first Memorial Cup, where he became the first player to win the CHL's player of the year award twice, cementing his status as one of the greatest juniors in hockey history.

"I just want to be known as a player who was honest every night, who shows up every night and never took anything for granted and played for the love of the game," Crosby said on awards night. "I have a passion for the game, and I try to show that every night I play."

Although Crosby dazzled the crowds for much of the tournament, he was effectively shut down by Perry's London Knights in the Memorial Cup final and wrapped up his Rimouski career with a second-place finish.

Crosby had arrived in Rimouski as an English-speaking kid who knew literally four words of French, but he left Rimouski two seasons later bilingual—handling French media interviews with ease—and fully prepared and determined to conquer the hockey world.

The NHL lockout soured a lot of people on the game, but Crosby's imminent arrival in the pros had all of the league's owners salivating that his star power would bring alienated fans back to their arenas. For the Pittsburgh Penguins—who won the right to select him by winning the lottery for the first pick in the 2005 draft—Crosby's arrival also gives them new hope of ending years of tumultuous financial problems. It remains to be seen if he has that ability, but it is certain that Crosby will enjoy every second he spends in the NHL, whether he turns into its greatest player or biggest bust. It's something his parents, and more specifically Troy, instilled in Crosby from day one.

"The minute you take things for granted," Crosby likes to say, "it can all be gone."

A Hall-of-Famer at 16

Ever since Sidney Crosby was a toddler, he dreamed of suiting up for Canada at the world junior hockey championships. When that dream finally came true in 2003, Crosby was only 16 years of age, still a toddler in hockey terms.

He came of age in Canada's second game of the tournament against an over-matched Swiss team. With the clock winding down in the third period of a game Canada was already leading 6–2, Crosby drove down the right wing with the puck, skipped over a diving Swiss defender, made a dramatic cut towards the net and roofed a sharp-angle wrist shot past Swiss goaltender Daniel Manzato with only 14 seconds left in regulation time. The meaningless goal made Crosby the youngest player—at 16 years, four months and 24 days—to score for Canada at the world juniors.

"It wasn't even anything I knew until after the game," Crosby said. "I never really think about age, but when they brought that up it was definitely pretty special."

It is widely believed Crosby became the youngest player to score for any team at the tournament, but the International Ice

Hockey Federation's statistics on the subject are not all that reliable. Hockey Canada public relations employee André Brin picked up the puck, just in case anyone wanted to hang on to the historic piece of rubber. And it's a good thing he did—today that puck sits in a display case at the Hockey Hall of Fame in Toronto.

Chapter Three

Marian Hossa

He was on the cusp of everything he had dreamed of. The start of a career in the NHL was at his fingertips; it was the completion of a difficult year where he had to battle homesickness and a language barrier, and there was nothing Marian Hossa wanted more than to score a goal.

It was the championship game of the 1998 Memorial Cup, and Hossa's Portland Winter Hawks and the Guelph Storm were tied 3–3 late in the third period with Canadian junior hockey supremacy riding on every shift. With just over five minutes left to play in regulation time, Winter Hawks coach Brent Peterson tapped the Western Hockey League's (WHL) rookie of the year on the shoulder, the player who had already given his team a goal and an assist in the game, and the 19-year-old Hossa jumped over the boards.

As Hossa crossed the ice, Guelph's Ryan Davis came out of nowhere and caught the talented winger with a vicious, and illegal, knee-on-knee hit. Hossa crumpled to the ice, writhing in pain. Although he didn't know it at the time, he had just torn the anterior cruciate ligament in his left knee, the one that controls forward motion, the one that controlled his future in the NHL.

He eventually got up, propped up on the shoulders of two teammates, and limped his way off the Spokane Arena ice. As Hossa received treatment from the team trainers, his teammates were in their dressing room getting ready to start overtime.

"The room was a little down without Hossa," Peterson said later. "He played wonderful and our guys just said, 'Let's do it for Marian.'"

At 6:21 of the extra frame, Portland's Bobby Russell put a rebound past Guelph goalie Chris Madden, and by the sound of the crowd, Hossa knew his team had just won the Memorial Cup. Although consumed by a combination of fear, doubt and pain, Hossa wasn't about to let this moment pass him by, not after everything he had gone through to get there. He limped his way back to the ice, sat down in an office chair and was carted around by his teammates to bask in the glory.

But as Hossa rested the historic Memorial Cup on his knee, he wasn't sure if he would ever get to compete at this level again, ever get to play the game he had loved essentially since birth, ever get to realize the lifelong dream of an NHL career. In a sense, his entire hockey-playing life flashed before his eyes.

Growing up in Trencin, a bustling textile town of 60,000 in the northeastern part of Slovakia, near the border of the present-day Czech Republic, Hossa and his younger brother, Marcel, were born into a family where only one thing mattered. "Hockey always came first," said their mother, Maria, "before everything else."

Their father, Frantisek, played defence for two years on the Czechoslovakian national team alongside the sibling trio of Peter, Anton and Marian Stastny—the first family of Slovakian hockey. Hossa first put on a pair of skates when he was about four years old, and whenever Frantisek's pro team had an optional skate, he took Marian and Marcel onto the ice with him.

Frantisek also helped his sons build a rink in the playground next to the family's two-bedroom apartment, using plywood stolen from a construction site to fashion a set of rudimentary boards. Building the makeshift rink was necessary because there was only one indoor arena in all of Trencin, and ice time was obviously hotly contested. Only the best and most promising young players were permitted on the ice, and it wasn't long before Hossa was one of those boys. From the beginning, Frantisek noticed his eldest son had extraordinary peripheral vision. He was able to find open teammates and spot oncoming defenders unusually well.

When Hossa was 10 years old, he sold his entire hockey card collection and used the money to buy a Wayne Gretzky instructional video for about $15. "A lot of money for a 10-year-old at that time," Hossa remarked. "You'd try some of his moves in practice, but then when you got in a game it was a different story."

Even if he was having trouble mastering The Great One's dekes right away, that video sowed the seeds of creativity and stickhandling that would become the strength of Hossa's game.

"Actually, I was not a great skater," Hossa admits. "[But] I was always able to score goals. I could stickhandle, but the skating was not as good as I want it to be."

Every year, between fifth and eighth grade, Hossa attended an elite hockey school with the best players in Trencin. At 16, he played for the Dukla Trencin junior team and racked up 42 goals and 49 assists. He played the next season on the first line for Dukla Trencin's senior team in the top Slovak professional league, skating against men in their 20s and 30s and scoring 25 goals with 19 assists in 44 games.

Hossa played in the 1997 world junior championships in Switzerland and scored 5 goals in six games for the sixth-place Slovakian squad. Ottawa Senators director of player personnel, Marshall Johnston, was scouting the tournament, and Hossa definitely caught his attention. Ottawa's head scout André Savard made several trips to Trencin that winter on Johnston's recommendation, and it wasn't long before he, too, became a Hossa fan.

At the 1997 NHL entry draft in June, Hossa was the second-rated European prospect behind Finland's Olli Jokinen. The Senators, sitting with the 12th pick, were elated to see that Hossa was still available when it came time for them to take the podium.

"He's talented," Savard said after drafting Hossa. "He has great hands, great vision. He's a very exciting hockey player."

That day marked the beginning of a challenging year for Hossa, one that saw him moving to a strange land at the age of 18 with only a few words of English in his vocabulary, but would also see his stock as a future NHL star shoot through the roof.

The media in Ottawa bombarded him with questions about his reputation for being a weak defensive player. But with his offensive display in his first NHL training camp, Hossa quickly made people forget about his supposed lapses on defence. In his first pre-season game, he got an assist and was a noticeable force all night. He finished the exhibition schedule with 7 points in seven games and, with star Senators winger Daniel Alfredsson holding out in a contract dispute, Hossa made the team to start the season.

"He's here to stay," head coach Jacques Martin said the day the final cuts were made. Martin's prediction barely lasted two weeks. Hossa managed just one assist in his first seven NHL games, and the Senators decided it was best if he played his first year in North America with the WHL's Portland Winter Hawks.

"The thing that I liked about Marian immediately was that he fit right into our team," Portland coach Brent Peterson said. "He's a very good hockey player, but even more than that he's a good personality. He works hard. He's not a crybaby and he doesn't worry about what's going wrong when he isn't playing well. He just comes back the next night and tries that much harder."

Junior hockey afforded Hossa a lot of time to learn English. With long bus rides a fact of life in junior hockey, Hossa slowly picked up the intricacies of English by watching movies and asking his teammates over and over again, "What did he say?"

"Some of our trips were 15 hours long," Hossa said. "You get to see a lot of movies."

On the ice, Hossa was learning another language as well, the North American hockey code. Although he had 9 points in his first 10 games with Portland, Hossa struggled to understand why players weren't getting penalties when they grabbed his arm or hooked his elbow. But most of all, for the life of him, Hossa couldn't understand why so many players refused to carry the puck into the offensive zone and opted instead for the safer dump-in. "It was like they didn't want to carry the puck and risk making a mistake," Hossa said.

In early December 1997, Hossa went back to Slovakia to try out for his home country's Olympic team that would go to Nagano, Japan. He then continued on to Finland for his second world junior championships where he notched 8 points in six games.

Hossa had been gone for almost a month, but when he returned to Portland, he picked up with the Winter Hawks exactly where he'd left off. He finished the 1997–98 season with 45 goals and 40 assists in 53 games to win the WHL's rookie of the year award and was named to the CHL's all-star team. It took Hossa a few games to adjust to playoff hockey in North America, where the line between legal and illegal play blurs even further than in the regular season.

"It was a new experience for him," Peterson said. "Instead of looking up at the referee, he had to learn how to fight through those checks."

He had only 6 goals in his first 12 playoff games, but in the league final, Hossa exploded for 7 goals in a four-game sweep of the Brandon Wheat Kings.

"He was just awesome," Brandon coach Bob Lowes said after the series. "Although he averaged almost two goals a game against us, he was getting

seven and eight great scoring opportunities a game...
When he saw a seam between two defencemen,
he would plow through it. He's so strong on the
puck. We couldn't handle him, and he killed us."

Hossa carried his momentum into the 1998
Memorial Cup, scoring 4 goals with 3 assists in
Portland's three round-robin wins to help the
Winter Hawks earn a bye directly into the final.
And then, with just over five minutes to play in
regulation time of a 3–3 hockey game, Guelph
Storm winger Ryan Davis took out his knee and
Hossa's whole career, everything he had worked
for, was suddenly in peril. As soon as he was able
to get to a phone after the 4–3 Portland overtime
win, Hossa called his parents to give them the bit-
tersweet news.

"We were here at home, in Trencin, waiting for
Marian to call and tell us if his team won," Maria
Hossa recalled. "He finally called, but his voice was
different. I thought maybe he had lost. He said, 'No,
we won, but I'm hurt.' I cried."

Three weeks later in Ottawa, with his parents
with him at the hospital, Hossa underwent successful reconstructive surgery to repair the torn anterior cruciate ligament in his left knee. That was the
good news. The bad news was that Hossa was star-
ing at four months of arduous rehabilitation, at
least. He attacked his rehab the same way he
attacked opposing nets. Senators strength coach
Randy Lee described Hossa's approach to his work-
outs as going "above and beyond what's normal."

While in Ottawa, Hossa befriended centre Radek Bonk, a Czech native, who helped him get further accustomed to life on this side of the Atlantic Ocean. "It was the first time I was living on my own," Hossa said. "I didn't know how to go to the bank and pay my bills. It doesn't sound like a big thing, maybe, but you need to have everything in your life [in order] so you can focus on your game."

Hossa wasn't allowed to step back on the ice until November, six months after the injury. "I have been in the gym so long," he said joyfully after the solo skate in Ottawa's Corel Centre. "I needed to feel cold." Finally, on December 5, 1998, he received permission from team doctors to play against the New York Rangers. Although he was held pointless on 16 shifts and 11:45 of ice time, Hossa's knee passed with flying colours. He was placed on the third line with Bonk and Magnus Arvedson almost immediately, and the trio quickly became regarded as the best third line in the league. "We went from a checking line to a checking line that could score," Bonk said. "That changed everything."

Hossa really turned it on in March, scoring 6 goals with 4 assists to be named NHL rookie of the month, giving him 15 goals and 15 assists on the year. He finished second to Colorado's Chris Drury in the 1998–99 Calder Trophy balloting despite missing 22 games while recovering from his surgery, and he was named to the league's all-rookie team.

During his first full season in the NHL the following year, Hossa finished third on the team in scoring with 29 goals and 27 assists, but a home game against the Toronto Maple Leafs on March 11, 2000, had a profound effect on the budding star's psyche. Hossa entered that game on a hot streak, with 9 goals in his previous 14 games, one of those zones where you feel everything you put on net will go in.

With less than five minutes to play in the second period, Hossa found a loose puck coming towards him in the Toronto end off a turnover and saw a scoring opportunity. Just as Maple Leafs captain Mats Sundin was slapping the puck out of the zone, Hossa spun around and wound up with a wild swing at the puck. Standing behind Hossa, unbeknownst to him, was Toronto defenceman Bryan Berard. As Hossa completed the follow-through on his ill-advised golf swing at the puck, the heel of his stick struck Berard directly in the right eye, rupturing it. Hossa went to the penalty box and sat there in a complete daze as trainers attended to Berard on the ice, wondering if he had just inadvertently blinded someone he had never even met. Berard was rushed to Ottawa General Hospital and was operated on for three and a half hours as doctors attempted to save the eye.

The following day, a nervous and repentant Hossa went to the hospital to see how Berard was doing and found his parents, Pam and Wally. They recognized him immediately. "He could hardly talk at the hospital," Wally Berard said. "He must have apologized to us four or five times."

As he walked up to Berard's hospital bed, Hossa's eyes welled up with tears as he struggled to find the appropriate words for the moment, if indeed there were any. Instead, he began to cry. If Berard had any resentment for Hossa, he didn't let it out then, or ever, for that matter.

"It was an accident, a freak accident. It could have been me doing it to you," Hossa remembers Berard saying. "He was a very strong man in the hospital. Very strong."

Despite getting Berard's gracious forgiveness, Hossa was not the same player he was before the accident. In the final 13 games of the 1999–2000 regular season Hossa scored only 2 goals, and he was kept completely off the scoresheet in Ottawa's six-game loss to the Maple Leafs in the first round of the playoffs. "I became less aggressive," Hossa said. "I was afraid to do something that might hurt someone. Hockey wasn't fun anymore."

Before leaving for Trencin that summer, Hossa phoned Berard, who told him again that he should get the accident out of his mind, that he needed to concentrate on hockey. In order to do that, Hossa decided it was best to get away from hockey.

He spent the summer playing tennis and hanging out with friends. It worked. Hossa came back for the 2000–01 season focused on hockey again, finishing second in team scoring with 32 goals and 43 assists. But, more importantly, he permanently shed his pre-draft reputation of being a one-dimensional player.

On November 18, 2000, Hossa was asked to kill a penalty for the first time in his Ottawa career. He not only killed off the penalty, he set a franchise record with two short-handed goals in the game, and his assist on another one by Bonk marked the first time the Senators had ever scored three times short-handed in one game. For good measure, Hossa added a power play goal in the same game for his first career hat trick. He was named to the all-star team that season, his first of three all-star selections over four seasons.

In 2002–03, Hossa set another Senators record with 45 goals, topping Alexei Yashin's 44-goal season of 1998–99. The bigger impact came with a goal he scored in the first game of Ottawa's second-round playoff series against the Philadelphia Flyers, where he dangled his way through the Flyers defence for an eternal 15 seconds before setting up centre Bryan Smolinski, which resulted in Hossa scoring on a rebound to tie the game 2–2. Flyers coach Ken Hitchcock said watching Hossa during that sequence made him dizzy.

Ottawa won that game and the series 4–2 before bowing out in game seven of the third round to the eventual Stanley Cup champion New Jersey Devils, marking an end to the Senators' deepest trip into the playoffs in modern team history.

That dizzying goal was more than just fodder for the sports highlight shows, it served notice to the league that Marian Hossa had overcome all the adversity that was strewn on his path and that he had officially arrived as an NHL star.

"It's year by year and step by step, a slow process, and the coach has to trust you," Hossa said. "And then, all of a sudden, you're in a game when you feel nobody can take anything from you, because you have the confidence to do it. That's what I had that game. I knew I could go around people and have control of the puck, and I felt I am able to do what I want to do."

And he's been doing it ever since.

The Sixth Sense

After watching Marian Hossa play for only one season, Ottawa Senators backup goaltender Ron Tugnutt thought he had the exciting Slovakian winger all figured out. Hossa was, quite obviously in Tugnutt's eyes, a psychic.

"You're tempted to say the puck follows him, but it doesn't," Tugnutt said before Hossa began his second year in Ottawa. "He knows where the puck is going to go. Talented players have a knack for that. They go to the open ice and find the puck. And if you give Hossa time with the puck, he's going to do some magnificent things with it. Who knows how good he can be? I'm just glad he doesn't read the papers so he doesn't see all the great things people say about him."

Those people have continued saying great things about him his entire career, just as Hossa keeps getting to the puck a half second before it gets there.

Chapter Four

Roberto Luongo

Florida Panthers general manager Bryan Murray was sitting at the 1997 NHL entry draft, biding his time until his team's 20th pick rolled around. He watched as one potential franchise player after another got snatched up by other teams. After the New York Islanders used the fourth selection on a lanky goaltender from Montréal by the name of Roberto Luongo, Murray longingly asked anyone within earshot, "Why can't we ever get players like that?"

Murray was not the only hockey type sitting in the Calgary Saddledome that day dreaming of Luongo guarding their net. By that point, all of 18 years old, Luongo had already established himself as a potential difference-maker, a goalie who could win games by himself. His reputation as an elite netminder at that age was certainly not misplaced; Luongo had accomplished more than enough to warrant the heavy praise. But it would certainly have been shocking to Luongo if anyone had told him when he began tending goal at the age of 11 that he'd one day have NHL general managers fawning over him seven years later.

Luongo, who grew up in the heavily Italian Montréal suburb of St-Leonard, was the eldest of Tony and Pasquelina Luongo's three sons. He was enrolled in the local minor hockey league when he was eight—very late for a Canadian kid. Although Luongo wanted desperately to play goal, his parents thought he should work on his skating as a forward first. He gave it a shot, playing on lower-level intercity teams for three years before being cut from his Atom CC team. It was only then, at the age of 11, that Luongo decided to take his shot between the pipes.

As the years went by, Luongo forgot the name of that coach who cut him in Atom, but he's grateful nonetheless. "It's thanks to him that I'm playing goalie," Luongo said.

It didn't take Luongo very long to climb into the upper echelon of up and coming Québec goalies, a status that is not easily attainable in a province that has produced more NHL goalies than any other place on earth. At the age of 15, Luongo went to play Midget AAA hockey for Montréal-Bourassa, a program that had already produced NHL netminders Martin Brodeur, Felix Potvin, Stéphane Fiset and Éric Fichaud, among others.

Luongo spent the 1994–95 season under the tutelage of Montréal-Bourassa goaltending coaches Mario Baril and François Allaire, the latter of which is widely credited with developing and fine-tuning the butterfly style made popular by Patrick Roy and copied by goalies worldwide. Luongo put together a solid rookie season with a 3.85 goals against average in 25 games in the high-scoring Québec midget AAA league, making him one of the most sought-after players for the 1995 Québec Major Junior Hockey League (QMJHL) draft.

Luongo's family didn't want to deprive their son of any opportunities, but they also didn't want him to completely depend on a hockey career. He was a strong student in high school, and U.S. colleges were already calling with scholarship offers. As the draft approached, Luongo and his parents came to an understanding. "We didn't think about hockey as a career then, I didn't know how far it could take him," Luongo's mother said. "We made a deal that if he was drafted in the first round, he'd go to juniors, and if he wasn't he'd wait for college. He was the second overall pick, so we didn't have a choice."

That pick was made by the Val D'Or Foreurs, making Luongo the highest-drafted goalie in QMJHL history, and it was quite possibly the best move in franchise history. Luongo was an instant success in Val D'Or, appearing in 23 games as a 16-year-old rookie and posting a solid 3.70 goals against with a 6–11–4 record.

Luongo set a franchise record in 1996–97 with 32 wins while allowing a scant average of 3.10 goals against in 60 games with a .901 save percentage, numbers nearly unheard of in the high-octane QMJHL. In the playoffs, he almost single-handedly led Val D'Or to a five-game playoff upset over the Memorial Cup champion Granby Prédateurs.

"He's the guy who has carried this team," Val D'Or general manager Michel Georges said during the playoffs. "He has been the inspiration for the rest of the guys. When we drafted him, we were looking for a guy who could carry the team in two years. He proved to everybody he could be that guy."

The most impressive asset of Luongo's game in the eyes of NHL scouts was his capacity to remain calm. Luongo never appeared the least bit bothered by anything, whether he allowed six goals or shut out the opposition. That calm was a result of all the responsibilities that Luongo had shouldered while growing up in St-Leonard.

"He's always been quiet, modest and mature," Luongo's mother said. "When he was young, his father and I owned a shoe store and there were many times when he had to leave him in charge of his two younger brothers or, with his father working so much, when he had to be the man of the house. He was very mature at a young age, he was almost like a second father."

Luongo was, and still is, a break from the conventional mold of elite goaltenders, almost exclusively smaller and therefore more agile and quick. But he was 6-foot-3, 180 pounds at the time, sporting size 15 feet. When he dropped down into his butterfly stance, it was almost as if he was casting an eclipse on the net, with just a thin outline of mesh visible to shooters.

"Roberto is the prototype goalie for the year 2000," Allaire said later. "He's got the perfect profile for today's NHL. He's different from a lot of the older goaltenders—he's got size, but for a big guy he's really athletic."

New York Islanders general manager Mike Milbury shared Allaire's assessment of the young Luongo, using his fourth overall pick to make him the highest-drafted goalie in NHL history in 1997, at the same time making Florida Panthers general manager Bryan Murray's mouth water.

Luongo was sent back to junior and had the best year of his young career. At the midpoint of the 1997–98 season, he was selected to serve as the backup goalie for Canada's entry to the world junior championships.

Canada finished a disappointing eighth at the worlds in 1998. After finishing Canada's 6–3 loss to lowly Kazakhstan in the seventh/eighth place game, Luongo sought out Hockey Canada director of scouting Barry Trapp, gave him a hug, and told him it would be a different story a year later.

"I knew right then and there who the number one goalie would be [in 1999]," Trapp said later.

Luongo returned to Val D'Or and led the Foreurs to the 1998 QMJHL championship and a berth in the Memorial Cup. In their opening game, Luongo was astounding, making 49 saves as Val D'Or lost 5–4 to the Spokane Chiefs. Even though his team didn't win a single game in the tournament, Luongo cemented his status as the next dominant product of the Québec goaltending factory.

At the 1999 national junior camp in Winnipeg, Luongo entered as the undisputed number one netminder, based largely on what he had told Trapp a year earlier. "This was his position to lose," Trapp said. "When he goes down into that butterfly, you tell me what part of the net you can see?"

Canada not only had the home-ice advantage in Winnipeg, they also had a decided advantage in nets. Luongo's play carried a pretty mediocre team—only by Canadian standards, mind you—to the championship final against Russia. He posted two shutouts, stopped a tournament-leading 94.2 per cent of the shots fired his way and allowed an average of 1.92 pucks to get past him per game.

Against Russia, Canada was smothered by a better-skating team, but thanks to Luongo, and a third period goal by Bryan Allen, they were able to finish regulation tied 2–2. But it didn't take the Russians long to claim the championship with a goal just

over five minutes into the overtime period, leading an exhausted and distraught Luongo to lie
motionless in his crease as the Russian team celebrated its victory right in front of the net.

As he skated up to centre ice to accept his award
as the tournament's top goaltender, Luongo had
tears in his eyes. "I'd trade the honours for the gold
medal," Luongo told reporters upon his arrival at
Montréal's Dorval Airport following the tournament. "I really wanted to win gold."

While Luongo was away with the national team,
the rebuilding Foreurs traded him to the Bathurst
Titan, and Luongo promptly led that team to the
1999 Memorial Cup.

The Islanders signed Luongo to a three-year contract shortly after watching him perform at the
world juniors, prompting Milbury to say, "In time,
we believe that he can be an elite goaltender."

Apparently, Luongo didn't progress fast enough
for Milbury's liking. Luongo spent the 1999–2000
season bouncing back and forth between the
Islanders and their American Hockey League affiliate, the Lowell Lock Monsters. Luongo's NHL
debut finally came on November 28, 1999, against
the Bruins in Boston, and it was one to remember.
Luongo stopped 43 shots that night to lead the
Islanders to a 2–1 win, providing a glimpse of what
he was capable of at the NHL level.

Yet Milbury continued antagonizing his young
star, once publicly questioning Luongo's decision to

spend the day looking for an apartment when he was supposed to play that night, and finally sending him back down to Lowell with Luongo one start short of earning a significant salary bonus.

A week before the 2000 draft, word spread that Milbury was looking to trade Luongo as he eyed Boston College standout Rick DiPietro to be the Islanders' new goalie of the future. Florida Panthers general manager, Bryan Murray, who had never forgotten watching Luongo step up to the podium in 1997, was quick to get Milbury on the phone. After a week of negotiations, Milbury selected DiPietro with the first pick overall, breaking his own record for the highest-drafted goalie in NHL history. Milbury then packaged Luongo and centre Olli Jokinen—who was drafted just before Luongo at third overall in 1997—to the Panthers for forwards Mark Parrish and Oleg Kvasha.

"As the draft progressed, it was clear that the value of Luongo was greater than the value of the first overall pick," Milbury explained to bewildered reporters. "We're rolling the dice a little bit. Roberto is going to be an excellent goaltender in this league. He's a class act and a kid we'd have been happy to ride with. But in our mind, if we could get DiPietro, he possessed an element that Roberto perhaps does not possess. He handles the puck as well as any goaltender in hockey today, not just any young prospect, anyone in any league anywhere."

For the Islanders, it went down as probably the worst trade in franchise history. For the Panthers, however, it was like winning the lottery without having to buy a ticket.

"Our scouts all know him, and they're all awfully excited right now," a beaming Murray said. "He's been excellent throughout his career...All I know is you don't get to the top level and win—or even compete—if you don't have a top goaltender."

Luongo was surprised at the move, considering he was never given a real shot at the number one job in Long Island, but he knew he would get that opportunity immediately in Florida. He took to his new spot on the Panthers roster with a new lease on his hockey life. He played in 47 games in 2000–01, compiled a 12–24–7 record for one of the worst teams in the league and had a sparkling 2.44 goals against average with five shutouts. His .920 save percentage was sixth best in the NHL that year and tied for second-best all-time for a rookie.

Luongo was selected to represent Canada at the 2001 world championships following the season, but his tournament was cut short when he broke the index finger on his right hand while stopping a slap shot. Armed with a new four-year contract, Luongo entered Panthers training camp in 2001 as the team's clear number one goalie. He put up the same kind of numbers, but his season ended in March after tearing a ligament in his right ankle.

In 2002–03, Luongo once again had a solid year for a bad Panthers team to earn another trip to the world championships. He never forgot his disappointment in losing the world junior final to Russia four years earlier. "That was a great experience, one of the best of my life," Luongo said at the start of the tournament. "If it wasn't for that goal in overtime, things would have been that much greater. I think about that a lot, especially when you're back here playing internationally. This is my chance to redeem myself and, hopefully, this year will be the one where I get the gold."

Luongo's words proved to be prophetic. Canadian starter Sean Burke pulled a groin in Canada's 8–4 semi-final win over the Czech Republic, so Luongo played the final against Sweden. After allowing two goals in the first period to fall behind 2–0, Canada rode Luongo's 37-save performance to a 3–2 win. Luongo had his redemption.

"After they scored their second goal I was a little mad, I told myself, 'I can't let any more in,'" Luongo said after receiving the gold medal. "Now I know what it feels like to be on the other side. It's a beautiful thing, a beautiful day for Canada."

Although the world championship gold medal proved Luongo could play in the big game, it wasn't until the 2003–04 season that his name was grouped with the best goalies in hockey. The Panthers were relying on a young and inexperienced defensive squad that year, and opposing forwards knew just how to take advantage. They peppered Luongo with a barrage of shots that season; they came from all angles and came in bunches.

Luongo played in his first all-star game that year, winning the goaltending portion of the all-star skills competition. By the end of the season, Luongo had faced 40 or more shots 15 times and had a 6–7–2 record in those games. His shutout total of 23 before his 25th birthday was one better than Martin Brodeur had at the same age. Even though Luongo set an NHL record with 2475 shots against and 2303 saves, his save percentage of .931 was still third best in the NHL.

"Not too many goalies make you have a meeting about the goalie, and he's one guy that you do," Philadelphia Flyers coach Ken Hitchcock said. "Psychologically, he can really get to people. He makes saves that border on unbelievable, and that becomes psychological after a while."

Luongo led Canada to another gold medal at the world championships in 2004, and his performance earned him a spot as the backup to Brodeur on Canada's entry in the World Cup of Hockey. Brodeur had sprained his left wrist in Canada's last round-robin game, which meant that Luongo would be in nets for the semi-final against the Czech Republic.

Luongo had been in the same situation two years earlier at the world championships, and the result this time was the same—Canada won

4–3 in overtime. Just like he did in the world championship gold medal game against Sweden, Luongo had a 37-save performance as Canada advanced to the final before dispatching Finland 3–2 to win the gold medal.

With those performances behind him, Luongo officially removed a tag that had followed him throughout his career. He was commonly known as the best young goalie in the NHL but that wasn't enough for Luongo.

"Forget young," Luongo once said. "Bottom line is, I want to be the best. That's it. I want to be the best in the world."

Hello, Bonjour, or Ciao—It's All the Same to Luongo

Roberto Luongo was born to an Italian immigrant father and an Irish-Canadian mother, so growing up he comfortably grasped French, English and Italian. Although Luongo left home at the age of 16 to play junior hockey, the Italian side of his heritage was never too far away.

In Val D'Or, Luongo spent two years as a billet with an Italian family there who he still keeps in touch with to this day. Once Luongo moved on to Miami, it didn't take him long to find another Italian family to take him in. A pizza restaurant in Coral Springs owned by Bobby Cerbone and Guy D'Aiuto quickly became Luongo's second home.

"They're my family," Luongo said. "I feel as comfortable with them as I do with my own family."

The gang at the Pizza Time Restaurant soon formed a fan club called Luongo's Legion, and they became well known as the rowdiest fans at Panthers games.

"There were about 30 of us, all Italian,"
Cerbone recalled. "One game we start
singing this soccer song, 'Ole, ole, ole, ole,'
and all of a sudden the whole arena joined
with us, and it was beautiful. Then it flashed
on the screen, 'Luongo's Legion is here.' So
they named us."

Chapter Five

Jarome Iginla

Jarome Iginla has had his doubters for most of his life. There were the kids in his Alberta hometown of St. Albert who didn't believe a black player could ever make the NHL; the Western Hockey League (WHL) scouts who ignored him in the bantam draft; the Calgary media who questioned the Flames' wisdom of trading Joe Nieuwendyk for an unknown commodity still in junior; the NHL officials who left his name off the all-star ballot; the Hockey Canada officials who only invited him to the Olympic orientation camp as a last-minute injury replacement; and, most notably, Jarome Iginla himself.

But in the end, Iginla has proved them all wrong. He's become the world's most complete and intimidating forward, someone who can provide his team with the big goal, the big hit, or even the momentum-turning fight.

Jarome Arthur Leigh Adekunle Tig Junior Elvis Iginla—the official name on his birth certificate— was a Canada Day baby, born on July 1, 1977, in Edmonton, Alberta. His father, Elvis Iginla, immigrated to Canada from Lagos, Nigeria, three years earlier and married an Oregon-born woman named Susan Schuchard, but the two divorced before Jarome's second birthday.

Schuchard raised Iginla as a single mother, with a lot of help from her parents, in the lily-white Edmonton suburb of St. Albert, though Iginla remains close with his father, an Edmonton-based lawyer. From an early age, even though he was a talented athlete who was the starting catcher for the Canadian Junior Baseball Team, Iginla's ambitions were firmly rooted in hockey. But as the son of a black Nigerian father and white American mother, few gave the youngster much of a chance of realizing his dream.

"As soon as I started playing hockey at the age of seven, I wanted to be an NHL player," Iginla said. "Sometimes, kids might say, 'There aren't very many black people in the NHL,' and I was aware of it. There weren't very many, but I followed how they all did...It meant a lot to me to be able to see other black hockey players in the NHL."

Schuchard knew she had to prepare her son for all the taunts and racially motivated slurs that would be sent his way as he navigated the minor hockey ranks. She taught him very early on that there was no way he could control what other people said or did, but the one thing he could control was the way he reacted.

Schuchard remembered a moment where it became evident that her son had taken in all of the advice she had given him. "It was another player," she said. "He couldn't tell the difference when Jarome had his helmet on, but when he took it off, the kid said, 'You're just a nigger.' Jarome just shrugged and shook his head."

Iginla also had the advantage of growing up as a huge fan of the Edmonton Oilers during their glory days of the 1980s. One of the pillars of that dynasty was the Oilers netminder, Grant Fuhr. Fuhr shared Iginla's mixed bloodlines and tinted skin colour and served as a wonderful inspiration for the young Iginla. "I remember saying, 'Look, there are black players, and Fuhr's not just playing, he's starring,'" Iginla said.

Iginla took that inspiration and ran with it. Although WHL scouts passed him over in the bantam draft, 15-year-old Iginla opened some eyes in Alberta by scoring 34 goals in 36 games for the St. Albert Saints in 1993. Later that fall he moved to Kamloops, BC, to play for the WHL's Blazers. The team's decision makers tried to ease the rookie into the system so he ended up languishing on the bench, or some nights, in the press box.

"I was on a very good team," Iginla says. "I felt I was as good as or better than some of the other young players in the league who were playing more on worse teams. It worked out in the long run, but it was difficult to take then."

Iginla posted 9 points in 19 playoff games for Kamloops that year as they won the WHL title before going on to win the 1994 Memorial Cup, the Blazers' first of two in a row. In 1995, after a 71-point season playing on a Memorial Cup–winning team that featured future NHLers Shane Doan, Darcy Tucker, Tyson Nash and others, Iginla was selected 11th overall in the NHL entry draft by the Dallas Stars. As if that wasn't sweet enough, the draft was held in Iginla's hometown of Edmonton, within earshot of all those kids who years earlier had told him there wasn't room for a black player in the NHL.

Iginla was on his way to the best season of his career with Kamloops when, on December 19, 1995, Dallas traded his rights along with goaltender Corey Millen to the Calgary Flames for star centre Joe Nieuwendyk. The day after the trade, a Calgary newspaper ran the headline "Jarome Who?" But it didn't take long for Flames fans to figure out exactly who Iginla was. He was their new franchise player.

A few weeks after the big trade, Iginla set about building his legend. He was named MVP for notching a tournament-leading 12 points in six games to lead Canada to the 1996 world junior championship in Boston, scoring the eventual game-winner against Russia in the gold medal

game. Upon his return to Kamloops, he put the finishing touches on a dominant season of 63 goals
and 73 assists for 136 points in only 63 games to
earn a spot on the Canadian Hockey League's first
all-star team. But the Blazers got knocked out in
the WHL playoffs, denying Iginla a third straight
trip to the Memorial Cup.

The same night that the Kamloops' season ended,
the Flames requested Iginla's presence in Calgary
the next morning, where they were playing game
three of their first-round playoff series with the
Chicago Blackhawks. Iginla woke up early the next
day and boarded a flight for Calgary, having no idea
what to expect, or why he was even going. He had a
quick meeting with Flames general manager Al
Coates and signed his first NHL contract about an
hour before the game. He then headed down to the
dressing room to join his new teammates, whom
only a day earlier he considered his heroes. The
whole process had happened so quickly that he
didn't even have time to get nervous.

Iginla was placed on the first line centring the
Flames' star winger Theoren Fleury and German
Titov, and he thrived almost instantly. He set up
a goal by Fleury and dropped the Blackhawks'
perennial all-star defenceman Chris Chelios with
a hard check, not once, but twice.

"The biggest thing is you go from watching the
NHL playoffs the night before, seeing the high-
lights, cheering for Calgary, watching Theo and

Trevor Kidd and Titov, cheering against Chelios and Ed Belfour. These are guys I'm looking up to one night wondering, 'Wouldn't it be awesome to play?'" Iginla said. "Because I don't know if I'm going to play an NHL game, ever. I want to. I'm planning on it. I'm dreaming of it. But you don't know when that day's going to be. Then, all of a sudden, it's literally overnight."

Although the Flames lost that game 7–5 to fall behind 3–0 in the series, Iginla had left his impression on his Flames teammates. "I remember after that game," Coates said, "Fleury coming over to me and telling me, 'That kid can play on my line any time.'"

Iginla scored the Flames lone goal in his second game on a low snap shot from the slot at 5:53 of the second period, but Calgary lost a triple-overtime marathon 2–1 as Chicago completed the sweep.

A few months later, on October 5, 1996, Iginla played his first regular season game in Vancouver and scored his first career goal, a great first step towards a solid rookie season of 21 goals and 50 points to finish second in the Calder Trophy balloting for rookie of the year honours. But what Iginla didn't know then was that game four against Chicago a year earlier was the last playoff game he would play for a long time, as the Flames embarked on a rebuilding program that kept them out of the post-season seven years in a row.

Iginla was the centrepiece of the Flames' youth movement, but his progression towards NHL stardom moved a little slower than Calgary would have liked. His goal total dropped to 13 in 70 games his sophomore season, but he rebounded with 28 goals in 82 games in 1998–99. Iginla's breakthrough came the following year when he posted career highs of 29 goals and 34 assists for 63 points, enjoying a 16-game point streak along the way. He improved slightly on those career marks in the 2000–01 season, but Iginla's best was yet to come.

In the late summer of 2001, Canada's best hockey players were converging on Calgary for the Olympic team's orientation camp. Iginla wasn't on the list of invitees, but since he didn't particularly feel he deserved to be there, he didn't take it as a slight. Then, Philadelphia Flyers forward Simon Gagné hurt his shoulder, and a spot suddenly opened up. Team Canada's executive director Wayne Gretzky—one of Iginla's boyhood idols— extended an invitation to the up-and-coming Flames forward. Gretzky called Iginla's then-fiancée Kara Kirkland (they were married in 2003) with the news, and when she told Iginla, he figured it was his Flames teammate Marc Savard pulling a prank. "I can just imagine pulling in there with all my equipment, and have them say, 'What does this guy think he's doing here?'" Iginla said.

Iginla's presence at the camp not only endeared him to the Team Canada executives in charge of selecting the team, it also erased any doubts he may have had about his place among the NHL's elite. "It's funny how things work out," Iginla said. "I'm sure one of the reasons I got to go to the camp at all was because it was in Calgary and I was in Calgary. Gagné got hurt and I was there, pretty handy, to fill in. And I can't tell you how much being there did for my confidence, seeing that I could keep up with all those stars. That really helped launch my season."

Iginla began the 2001–02 season with his second career "Gordie Howe Hat Trick"—one goal, one assist and one fight—in a 4–2 road win over the daunting Red Wings at Detroit. In fact, Iginla had 2 assists in that game.

Then in October, in a 3–1 win over the Florida Panthers, Iginla embarked on a 15-game points streak during which he scored a whopping 18 goals with 13 assists for 31 points to take a stranglehold on the league scoring race that he would never relinquish.

Although Iginla's performance that season— 52 goals and 96 points—earned him the Lester B. Pearson MVP Trophy as voted by the players, his breakthrough moment came at the Salt Lake City Olympics in February 2002. He scored his first goal of the tournament in Canada's 7–1 whipping of Belarus in the semi-final. But in the gold medal game against the host United States, Iginla's line with Joe Sakic and Gagné was easily the most dominant on the ice.

Iginla gave Canada a 2–1 lead in the first period, driving hard to the net and fighting off a Brian Leetch check to convert a beautiful cross-ice feed from Sakic. The U.S. tied it 2–2 in the second, but Sakic restored Canada's lead before the end of the period with a power play goal from the point. The third period was some of the best hockey ever played, as the Americans tried desperately to tie the contest as the clock continued to tick down towards a Canadian victory.

Iginla iced the game for Canada with just under four minutes left when his shot from the slot bounced off the trapper of U.S. goalie Mike Richter and flew up in the air, eventually bouncing behind Richter and slowly trickling across the goal line.

The line combined for 8 points between them to lead the charge in a 5–2 victory that broke a 50-year Olympic drought for the Canadian hockey program and sent Iginla on the road to superstardom.

"Looking back, it's the final game that I'll remember the most," Iginla said on the one-year anniversary of the gold medal win. "The game was so intense. I didn't think about winning or losing until the last three minutes. That's when I thought, 'We're going to have this.' It was just the best feeling."

As great as that feeling was, Iginla experienced more success in the 2003–04 season that would rival his Olympic euphoria. His Calgary Flames—who still hadn't played a playoff game since Iginla was a teenager—finally squeaked their way into the post-season tourney in 2004 despite a subpar second half of the season. Iginla started that season very slowly, but he rebounded to finish the year tied for the league-lead in goals with 41. In the playoffs, however, Iginla took his game to new heights. Every time Calgary needed a big goal, Iginla answered the call. He scored twice in game seven of Calgary's first-round series against the Vancouver Canucks and set up Martin Gelinas' series-winning goal in overtime.

In the second round against the high-powered Red Wings, Iginla helped create Calgary's only goals in a pair of 1–0 wins that gave the Flames the series in six games. Against the San Jose Sharks in round three, he scored the first goals in Calgary's 3–0 win in game five and its 3–1 series-clinching win in game six.

By the time the Flames had reached the Stanley Cup final against the Tampa Bay Lightning, Iginla had game-winning points in half of Calgary's 12 playoff wins. In game five of the final, with the series tied 2–2, Iginla had what his centreman Craig Conroy called "the greatest shift I've ever seen." With just over five minutes to play in the first overtime of a 2–2 hockey game, Iginla lost his helmet early in the shift, nearly set up a goal with a backhand pass, backchecked to win the puck back for Calgary, motored back up ice and unleashed a mammoth slap shot on Lightning goalie Nikolai Khabibulin. The rebound was too much for Khabibulin to handle, and Oleg Saprykin banged home the rebound to give Calgary the win and a 3–2 series lead.

Even though the Flames lost the next two games and the series, Iginla cemented his status as one of the NHL's next great poster boys. He can light up the scoresheet, drop the gloves, drive you into the boards, give a great interview and still sign every autograph requested of him afterwards. In short, his doubters have been silenced for good.

Need a Room?

Jarome Iginla's strengths are well documented, but if he has one weakness, it may be that he is too nice. Iginla was dining at a Salt Lake City eatery with his extended family during the Olympics when his waitress told him there were four men from Calgary sitting at another table. Iginla got up, walked over to their table and sat down for a little 10-minute powwow. The four men had driven down from Calgary to Utah and bought some tickets from a scalper to watch Canada play the Czech Republic during the round-robin portion of the tournament.

Since hotel rooms in Salt Lake City were completely non-existent, the four men were sleeping in their car in the parking lot of a local hotel. Having heard their tale, Iginla got up and went back to his family. A few minutes later, he returned to tell the guys he had booked them in the local Marriott Courtyard, and he even wrote down some directions to the hotel. When the fans from Calgary checked out of the hotel the next day, they found out that Iginla had not only secured the reservation, he had paid the $250 for the room as well.

Chapter Six

Zdeno Chara

Z deno Chara was considered a throw-in, an appendage to a trade that was bigger than him, even though he was the biggest player in NHL history. The main attractions of the draft-day deal on June 23, 2001, were Alexei Yashin, who sat out the entire year in a contract dispute with the Ottawa Senators, and Jason Spezza, a heavily-hyped super-prospect with franchise player potential.

Chara, to that point in his career with the New York Islanders, was considered by most hockey fans as a novelty act, a 6-foot-9, 255-pound Goliath on skates. That reputation was perpetuated by the Islanders' coaching staff, who insisted Chara concentrate only on playing mistake-free and clearing bodies away from the front of his net. Rushing up ice, or carrying the puck for that matter, was extremely frowned upon. So Chara's inclusion in the blockbuster trade that sent Yashin to the

Islanders for winger Bill Muckalt and the second pick in the draft, which the Senators used to get Spezza, was hardly headline material.

But what nobody knew then—and what everybody knows now—was that the throw-in would be the most valuable piece of that deal.

"When I compare Yashin and Chara," said the engineer of that trade, former Senators general manager Marshall Johnston, less than two years later, "I like that deal one-for-one."

It was never easy for Chara to shed the label of simply being a big defenceman. Of course, when you're seven feet tall in skates and use a stick that's six feet long, it's not an easy reputation to shake. His parents, Zdenek and Viktoria Chara, were hardly short at 6-foot-2 and 5-foot-9, respectively, but they weren't exactly ducking to get through doors.

As a boy growing up under communism in the Slovakian textile town of Trencin, Chara helped his family tend to their animals, but he was also being groomed to become an elite athlete.

Chara's father, a Greco-Roman wrestler who represented the former Czechoslovakia at the 1976 Montréal Olympics, put the 13-year-old Chara under a training regimen. The boy worked out three times a day; he ran before breakfast, lifted weights after breakfast and cycled at night. "Many times, he pushed me so hard that I ended up crying," Chara said years later. "I would wonder why he was so mean to me, but I didn't understand what he was trying to do. He meant it in a good way."

Chara was a reasonably big teenager for his age, but when he was 16 years old he shot up six inches to 6-foot-6. All of a sudden he was unusually huge. "I remember one night," his father said, "he called me into his room and told me that he could feel his thighs growing."

Chara didn't adapt very quickly to his new stature, and it showed on the ice. "It was a very tough time for me," he said. "I was growing so fast my coordination couldn't keep up."

Hockey coaches in Slovakia, most particularly in Trencin, were accustomed to players who had speed and skill. Trencin is home to such NHL snipers as Marian Hossa, Marian Gaborik and Pavol Demitra, among others. Faced with such a unique case as Chara, Trencin's hockey coaches didn't really know what to make of the gangly teenager, or what to do with him. Players with size were less coveted in Europe because the large international ice surface— about 3000 square feet bigger than a North American rink—made speed a more valuable trait than brute force. Almost every Slovakian player that made the NHL played forward, and the country had never produced a single star defenceman.

Most everyone encouraged Chara to forget hockey and concentrate on a sport where his height would be more useful—basketball. But when Chara ripped down the rim while dunking a ball at his neighbourhood school, he was no longer welcome to play that either. So Chara continued playing hockey, despite all his detractors.

At 17, Chara played Junior B hockey for Trencin, but by then he was so big that finding equipment that fit him became a real challenge. Chara's shin pads were too short and his shoulder pads so small they were almost useless. Worse still, Chara played the second half of that season with one skate blade separated from the boot. Since he was playing such a low level of hockey, he wasn't a priority case for new equipment in Trencin, so Chara used duct tape to hold his skate together. "It wasn't too bad," Chara recalls. "I wanted to play, so I made the best of the situation. It was no big deal."

The Islanders, despite Chara's lack of experience, were impressed enough with his size to take him with the 56th pick of the 1996 NHL entry draft. All of a sudden, Chara, never even selected to play on his own junior national team, was being given a chance. But he couldn't see himself taking full advantage of that opportunity playing at home, where no one believed he should be playing hockey in the first place, so Chara moved to Canada to play with the Prince George Cougars of the Western Hockey League (WHL).

"If I had stayed [in Slovakia], I probably wouldn't be playing hockey today, I'm sure," Chara later said. "It was probably the best thing that happened to me."

Although Trencin's coaches had no idea how to take advantage of Chara's dimensions, he was a coach's dream in the rough and tumble WHL. Chara still needed to work on his mobility, but there was no one who could challenge him physically and get away with it.

"Zee was a lot different than other guys, so if you tried to measure him using all the usual standards, you could think this guy could never play," said Stan Butler, Chara's coach in Prince George. "But he would do things that wouldn't just surprise you, they'd shock you."

The smaller North American rinks suited Chara's game to perfection, allowing him to better use his reach and sparing him the chore of having to chase darty forwards when he could just drill them into the boards instead. He also gained a reputation as one of the league's best fighters, using his leverage to throw tough guys around like rag dolls. "Because my dad was a wrestler, he taught me very early how to protect myself, to stand up for myself," Chara said. "He knew how to prepare me."

After helping the Cougars make a decent run in the 1996–97 WHL playoffs, Chara signed a three-year contract with the Islanders and, after some grooming in the minors, made his NHL debut in Detroit on November 19, 1997.

Over the following two seasons Chara showed significant improvement. The Islanders preached simplicity to their new defenceman, and he followed their every word, chipping the puck off the glass and out of his zone whenever he got the chance. In 1998–99, officially his rookie season, Chara averaged 18:54 of ice time per game while leading the Islanders in hits and finishing fourth on the team in blocked shots. At the end of the season Chara's talent was finally validated by the Slovakian national hockey program when he was invited to play in the world championships, the first time he represented his country in international competition. It soon became a habit.

Chara played for Slovakia again in the 2000 world championships and helped lead the team to a silver medal, the best result ever for the tiny country of about 5.5 million people. The team's performance caused such a frenzy that Slovakian Prime Minister Mikulas Dzurinda made a surprise trip to St. Petersburg, Russia, to watch the final—a 5–3 loss to their Czech rivals—and the country hired two private jets to fly the team home, where their adoring public awaited them.

Chara appeared to have gained confidence with Slovakia's performance and showed up for training camp in the fall of 2000 ready to make his mark in the NHL. Although the Islanders were still curtailing Chara's burgeoning offensive abilities, he displayed improved consistency. He averaged 22:20 of ice time in playing all 82 games that year, one of only three Islanders players to do so, and he led the NHL with 373 hits.

The next spring, as Chara was relaxing at home in Trencin after his third straight world championship appearance, he got a phone call informing him that he had been traded to the Ottawa Senators. Although he didn't know it at the time, the trade would give his hockey career a massive boost.

The Senators had just suffered their third straight elimination in the first round of the playoffs. It was the second year in a row the Toronto Maple Leafs had knocked Ottawa out in the first round, and the second time in three years the Senators failed to win a single playoff game. In short, the Senators were widely seen as the softest team in the NHL.

Chara was perfectly suited to toughen the Senators up, while Ottawa also managed to get some offensive talent in return for Yashin by drafting Spezza. In essence, Ottawa got the top North American prospect in the draft and the biggest player in NHL history in exchange for someone who didn't play a single game for the Senators all season. Although the general public wasn't making much of Chara's move to the Senators, his new teammates couldn't have been happier to welcome their hulking new defenceman. For Marian Hossa, who grew up a few blocks away in Trencin, being boyhood friends didn't change the fact that Chara made his life painful whenever he attempted to go anywhere near the net.

"I'm a lot happier that he's on my team," Hossa said in the weeks following the deal. "I've talked to Marty [Havlat] and Radek [Bonk] too, and they're pleased they don't have to go against him anymore."

Chara thought he knew exactly why Ottawa traded for him, and as soon as he arrived he began talking up his strength. "I like to play physical, to make it really uncomfortable for the other team's top players to play against me," he said. "That's my game."

Except that Ottawa's front office had seen something in Chara that the Islanders never did: a major offensive weapon. Head coach Jacques Martin emancipated Chara from his chains, encouraging him to rush the puck if he saw an opening, and eventually moving him onto the power play to act as a gargantuan screen in front of the goalie. The first time Chara filled that role for Ottawa, he scored a goal to end a five-game string where Ottawa went 1-for-17 with the man advantage.

Chara thrived on all the new responsibility. In his first season in Ottawa he scored 10 goals, four more than in his 231 previous NHL games combined. He also set new career marks with 13 assists, 23 points, 4 power play goals, 2 game-winning goals and a plus-30 defensive rating, the best on the team and fifth best in the NHL.

"When we saw him before with the Islanders, we knew that what he brought was the physical dimension," said Senators captain Daniel Alfredsson, after about half a season playing with Chara.

"But he's mobile, he's good with the puck and he doesn't panic. I think we've really been surprised with his skill."

Finally, for the first time in his life, let alone his career, Chara was being judged on something other than just his size.

But in February 2002 Chara had one of the biggest disappointments of his life at the Olympics in Salt Lake City. Because Slovakia was a relative newcomer on the international scene, and despite their silver medal at the 2000 world championships, they had to play in a tournament to qualify for the Games. The problem was that the qualification tournament took place while the NHL schedule was still on, so nearly all of the Slovakian players had to miss at least one of their NHL games if they wanted to play in all the Olympic qualifiers, something none of their teams would allow.

Hossa and Chara were released by the Ottawa Senators to play in Slovakia's second qualification game against Latvia. With a 3–0 loss to Germany already in the books, the Slovakians had to beat Latvia and then Austria if they wanted any shot at the main draw.

Hossa and Chara played a game against the Detroit Red Wings, then got on an overnight flight to arrive in Salt Lake City at 6 AM, the morning of the Latvia game. The two players went straight to their hotel room and slept until noon when they heard a knock on the door. Chara opened the door and saw Slovakian general manager Peter Stastny standing there with head coach Jan Filc. They had bad news.

Because Washington Capitals star Peter Bondra was available for Slovakia's game against Austria, Stastny and Filc needed to keep a roster spot open for him to play. Since neither Chara nor Hossa were released by the Senators to play against Austria, one of them would have to sit out against Latvia, and it was deemed Hossa would be more valuable in the game than Chara.

Once again Chara was being left out because he did not fit the mold of the ideal Slovakian player. It was akin to being left at an Olympic altar. But Chara took the snub, only the latest in a long line of them from his native country, like a man. A bigger man than most.

"There's nothing I can do about it," Chara said hours after hearing the bad news. "We can only have so many players, and because we lost [against Germany], we have to win the next two games... I wanted to attend the Olympics, to do the best for my country. On the other hand, sometimes you have to sacrifice. They made the decision. I respect it. It's fine."

Upon his arrival back in Ottawa, Chara prepared for the biggest test of his hockey life—playing in the first playoff game of his career. Senators fans couldn't wait. For years they had watched as their hockey team got pushed around like little boys being bullied at recess, and they were all counting on Chara to make that a thing of the past. But it wasn't only the fans; having Chara wearing their jersey gave the Senators a newfound sense of physical confidence. It was as if each of the players had put on 10 pounds by his mere presence.

"He's going to enjoy this, he's a playoff type of guy," Hossa said just before the Senators were to take on the big and tough Philadelphia Flyers. "You don't have to be afraid with him at your back."

The Flyers weren't particularly concerned about the Senators, relying on the old perception of how to eliminate Ottawa in the first round. "All we have to do," Flyers enforcer Donald Brashear said before the series, "is play them physical."

But Chara made some of Philadelphia's biggest forwards eat Brashear's words. Ottawa lost the first game of the series, but then went on to win the next three by identical 3–0 scores, and Chara's presence started to wear on the Flyers stars. "Oh my God," Philadelphia centreman Jeremy Roenick said, "with his wingspan and size, it's like he's about 13 feet long."

The Senators took game five 2–1 in overtime to make it past the first round for the first time in four years, earning them a date with their annual spring dance partners—the hated Toronto Maple Leafs. The Senators were really going to find out if their off-season deal would bear fruit. Ottawa won 5–0 on the road in game one, but the Maple

Leafs came back to knot the series at one with a 3–2 win. The two teams then split the next two games in Ottawa to send it back to Toronto tied two games apiece.

The winner of game five would take a stranglehold on the series. If the Senators could pull it off, they would have a chance to win the series back at the Corel Centre in front of their fans who had been subject to much heartache at the hands of the Leafs.

The Senators jumped out to a 2–1 lead going into the third period but allowed the tying goal with just under eight minutes to play. Moments before Alfredsson scored the game-winning goal for Ottawa, Chara attempted what looked to be a very casual play by pinching in off the blue line to keep the puck in the Toronto zone. Just after making the play, however, Chara was hit by the Maple Leafs Alyn McCauley and immediately left the ice.

The next morning, what had been a jubilant team was suddenly downtrodden with the news that Chara had a strained medial collateral ligament in his knee and would miss the final two games. The single most dominant factor in the series would no longer be with them out on the ice. If Chara's importance to the Senators was ever questioned, it was quickly answered when Ottawa lost game six at home 4–3 and fell completely flat in getting shut out 3–0 in Toronto in game seven, marking the third straight year the Leafs knocked the Senators out of the playoffs.

Although the series was negative for the Senators as a team, it was a coming-out party for Chara. The next season he was named to the 2002–03 Eastern Conference all-star team, and the following year he was named an NHL first-team all-star and finished second to New Jersey's Scott Niedermayer in the Norris Trophy voting for the league's best defenceman.

This was the kid who wasn't meant to play hockey, who was supposedly better off on a basketball court, who was apparently too slow and goofy to ever master the game.

But he has done just that.

A Prince George Van-Owner's Dream

When Zdeno Chara, all 6-foot-9 and 255 pounds of him, first arrived in Prince George, BC, to play major junior hockey with the Cougars, he didn't have a whole lot of money. Cougars coach Stan Butler was an influential figure in Prince George, and he persuaded a local car wash owner to give the young Chara a job.

"I went by a week later and asked the owner how he was making out," Butler recalled. "He says [Chara] was the best employee he ever had. He was the only guy who ever worked there who didn't need a ladder to clean the roof of a van."

Chara's size, however, wasn't always as appreciated by the town folk. Chara was placed with a billet family in Prince George. Before long, Butler received a phone call from Chara's hosts. "They said they were open to having another player," Butler said, "but on the allowance that we were giving billets, they could not afford to feed Zee."

Chara admits that his appetite is bigger than most, but that's only natural seeing as the man's *everything* is bigger than most. But he insists his stomach was not the only one driving a hole in his hosts' wallets. "I was there with another player who was about 220 pounds," Chara said in his defence. "We both ate a lot."

Chapter Seven

Dany Heatley and Ilya Kovalchuk

Dany Heatley and Ilya Kovalchuk both insist they hit it off as soon as they met at their first rookie camp in 2001 with the Atlanta Thrashers. But the first time they met on the ice at the 2000 World Junior Hockey Championships in Moscow, Heatley was not one of Kovalchuk's biggest fans.

With Russia clinging to a 2–1 lead late in the third period of a preliminary round game, and the Canadian net empty in favour of an extra skater, Kovalchuk picked up the puck at his own blue line with an unfettered path to the net at the other end of the ice. Heatley, playing for Canada, was a few metres behind Kovalchuk, trying in vain to catch up to the speedy winger. Heatley's position provided him with a great view of Kovalchuk who, after crossing the Canadian blue line, took one hand off his stick and pumped his fist in celebration *before* calmly sliding the puck into the gaping net to give Russia an insurmountable 3–1 lead over their biggest hockey rivals.

Although the loss was a disappointment to a nation of hockey fans, it was Kovalchuk's hasty celebration that caught the ire of the Canadian players and those who were supporting them back home. As Kovalchuk continued to dance around the ice in ecstasy, Heatley didn't find the move particularly amusing. "Not at the time," a smiling Heatley said about a year after the tournament. "Some guys obviously were a little mad."

But by this point, Heatley had half a season under his belt playing on the same line as Kovalchuk with the Thrashers, giving him a front-row seat for his linemate's animated goal celebrations. "If you're on the other team, you don't want to see that," Heatley continued, "but when he's on your team, that's what you want."

Heatley's and Kovalchuk's simultaneous arrival to the Thrashers in 2001 was like hockey's version of the perfect storm—two powerful forces converging on the same place at the same time. Heatley was Atlanta's first-round pick in the 2000 draft, going second overall after the New York Islanders selected goaltender Rick DiPietro. But the Calgary native went back to the University of Wisconsin for his sophomore season, where he was nominated for the Hobey Baker Award as U.S. college player of the year in 2001, but lost out to another goaltender, Buffalo Sabres prospect Ryan Miller of

Michigan State University. Kovalchuk came to Atlanta as a hot-headed 18-year-old who had just finished two seasons playing in the Russian Elite League and was the first Russian to be selected with the number one overall pick in the NHL draft.

Although their two personas seemed completely incompatible, Heatley and Kovalchuk became fast friends after rooming together at the Thrashers rookie camp in Michigan.

The pair of young stars came from similar sports environments. Heatley's father, Murray, played professionally in the World Hockey Association and in Germany, where he met Heatley's mother, Karin. Heatley was born in Freiburg, Germany, in 1981. Murray had his son in skates by the age of three, and Heatley often tagged along to his dad's practices and games. By the time Heatley and his family moved to Calgary just after his fourth birthday, he was already bitten by the hockey bug.

Kovalchuk's father, Valeri, played professional basketball in Russia's first division in the city of Tver, not far from Moscow. Kovalchuk was taken to the gym by the time he was three years old to work on stretching and coordination. When he was five years old, his dad looked out the window and watched as his son played ball hockey. He saw it right then and there. His son would be a hockey player.

So both of the youngsters had been groomed for this moment almost since birth, and therefore all eyes were on Heatley and Kovalchuk as the Thrashers real training camp began in the fall of 2001. Kovalchuk had blazing speed, enough size to play a rugged game and an incredible knack for being able to shoot a puck while skating at top speed without having to glide to line up his shot. Heatley was a physical presence with good ice vision and pillow-like hands, who was at his best between the faceoff circles and the net.

Heatley and Kovalchuk didn't wait very long to give Atlanta fans a taste of their potential, each of them scoring two goals in their first pre-season game. Kovalchuk finished that exhibition season as the team's top scorer with 6 goals and 4 assists in six games, and Heatley grabbed 3 goals and 1 assist playing on the opposite wing.

Once the regular season began, however, it was Heatley who was most at ease among the pros. It was to be expected, since Heatley played two years in college, but he still exceeded the Thrashers hopes by getting at least a point in 9 of his first 13 games.

Kovalchuk, on the other hand, was having trouble grasping the North American hockey code. The first three penalties of his NHL career were for diving. His play in his end of the rink, an area he almost never ventured to in Russia, was a liability in the NHL. Thrashers coach Curt Fraser didn't want to limit his young star's obvious offensive talents, but he also couldn't have one of his players floating around outside the blue line while the rest of his team was pinned in their zone.

In early November of the 2001–02 season, Fraser benched Kovalchuk one game for missing two crucial defensive assignments that led to 2 goals in a 4–1 loss. "He has habits from other places, and we work with him every day to break those," Fraser said in explaining his move. "I'm not going to turn this kid into a third-line checker. As he plays, we can teach him defense."

By this point, however, Kovalchuk's offensive flair was beginning to show, while Heatley was consistently producing at an alarming rate. The league took notice of them at the YoungStars game during all-star weekend when Kovalchuk pumped in six goals and added an assist to win the game's MVP award. It became increasingly obvious that the NHL Calder Trophy for rookie of the year was going to one of the two Thrashers rookies. Heatley and Kovalchuk were riding one-two in the rookie scoring race when, with 16 games left in the season, Kovalchuk dislocated his right shoulder and was out for the rest of the year.

Although he still finished in first place among NHL rookies with 29 goals, missing the end of the season cost Kovalchuk any shot at winning the award, as Heatley was on his way to a 26-goal, 41-assist campaign. Heatley received 48 of the 62 first-place votes in the balloting, while Kovalchuk received the other 14 to finish second. The following year Heatley and Kovalchuk didn't skip a beat, improving their play after the arrival of new head coach Bob Hartley midway through the 2002–03 season.

During all-star weekend, it was Heatley's turn to make a statement. Playing with the big boys this time, Heatley scored 4 goals through two periods to tie the record for most goals in an all-star game. During the second period, Heatley was paid a visit by one of the holders of that record, Wayne Gretzky. "Don't stop at four," Gretzky told him. "Get six or seven, something you'll be proud of for a long time."

Heatley did get one more goal, but it didn't officially count as it came during a shootout, but he was still a no-brainer pick as the game's MVP even though his Eastern Conference team lost. Heatley finished the season with a team-best 41 goals and 48 assists while Kovalchuk had 38 goals and 29 assists.

Kovalchuk was still struggling with his defensive responsibilities and Hartley treated his lapses with tough love, letting him steam on the bench any time he had a miscue in his own end. But Hartley didn't mind as much as it seemed. Defence can be taught, but Kovalchuk's skills are not covered by any chapter in the coaching manual. "Kovy and I are like father and son," Hartley said soon after another Kovalchuk benching. "I'd rather try to slow down a thoroughbred than try to kick a donkey to get going."

The Thrashers were improving at the same rate as the two young superstars, and Hartley's arrival as coach actually triggered a late-season run to the playoffs in 2003 that came up just short. But the momentum at the end of the season was a source of great optimism in the Thrashers' front office for the first time in the franchise's short history.

Just before the start of the 2003–04 season that hope was shattered by a tragic accident. While Heatley was driving teammate Dan Snyder home from a team function in suburban Atlanta in his black Ferrari sports car, he came upon a winding road with a stone wall bordering one side of it. Travelling more than double the speed limit at about 130 kilometres per hour, Heatley crashed the car into the stone wall, thrusting his friend from the vehicle. Snyder succumbed to the massive brain injuries six days later. Heatley survived the accident, suffering torn anterior cruciate and medial collateral ligaments in his right knee, breaking his jaw, bruising a kidney and damaging his left shoulder. But more painful than any of those wounds was the guilt he felt for the loss of his dear friend Snyder.

"I'm going to deal with this forever," he said months later. "Every time I go to sleep I think about Dan. It'll be with me for the rest of my life...As a person, I'll never be the same."

Heatley was already in line to face a number of criminal charges, but when Snyder died, one count of first-degree vehicular homicide was added. Snyder's parents, however, did not want Heatley to go to jail and immediately came out in support of their son's good friend. The Snyders' support and compassion went a long way towards Heatley's eventual plea agreement to serve three years probation with 750 hours of community service.

From the standpoint of the Atlanta Thrashers, the accident was an emotional blow, but it also suddenly increased Kovalchuk's importance in the team's success. Starting his first season without Heatley, Kovalchuk got off to a torrid start, being named NHL player of the month for October with 11 goals and 6 assists as Atlanta lost only three of its first 11 games of the season.

While Kovalchuk was ripping up the NHL, Heatley was attempting to recover from his physical and, most importantly, emotional scars. The reconstructive knee surgery Heatley underwent usually takes four to six months of recovery time, but less than three months later he was back on his skates. On January 28, 2004, close to four months after the accident, Heatley played his first game with the Thrashers, returning to a standing ovation from the fans at Philips Arena. As Heatley lined up to take the opening faceoff, St. Louis Blues forward Keith Tkachuk lined up opposite him and whispered a few words. "I told him we were thinking about him—me, our entire team, the league," Tkachuk said. "[I] just wanted to give him support. He's an exceptional person...and it's important that he was just out there."

Although it took him a few games to shake off the rust, Heatley finished the season strongly with points in 18 of his final 24 games to finish with 13 goals and 12 assists in 31 games.

Kovalchuk, meanwhile, put the finishing touches on his best season yet, tying the Columbus Blue Jackets Rick Nash and Calgary Flames Jarome Iginla for the league-lead with 41 goals. Heatley continued his season playing for Canada at the 2004 world championships and proved that the horrible accident was behind him, leading the tournament with 8 goals and 11 points to claim MVP honours and lead Canada to its second straight gold medal.

But Heatley faltered somewhat in the subsequent World Cup of Hockey and 2005 world championships, and before the start of the 2005-06 season he ended his dream partnership with Kovalchuk.

Heatley asked the Thrashers for a trade so he could give himself a fresh start as he continued to recover from the emotional scars of the accident, and Waddell obliged by sending him to the Ottawa Senators for star winger Marian Hossa and defenceman Greg DeVries.

Just like that, the perfect storm had been calmed.

Chapter Eight

Jose Theodore

It was the blocker-save heard around the world. The Montréal Canadiens were desperately clinging to a 2–1 lead with just under half a period left to play in the sixth game of their 2002 opening-round playoff series with the Boston Bruins. The Canadiens had no business even being in the playoffs, let alone in a position to oust the top-seeded Bruins. But here they were on the verge of advancing to the second round thanks solely to the brilliant play of their man in nets, the local kid made good, Jose Theodore.

Boston, however, wasn't about to go away quietly. They had taken the play to Montréal throughout the third period of game six, if not the entire series, and were buzzing around Theodore's net looking for the tying goal that could salvage their season. Boston's formidable bookends, power wingers Glen Murray and Bill Guerin, had posted themselves so close to Theodore they could smell him. Meanwhile, their Bruins teammates feverishly tried to get anything and everything at the net.

Suddenly, Murray was all alone in front of Theodore, but his shot got stopped by a lightning quick pad shooting out to intercept it. Moments later, a Bruins shot got through a crowd and past Theodore but clanged off the post. The puck lay in the crease, a little tap away from the Montréal goal line, and Guerin's eyes lit up in anticipation as he saw it sitting there within his reach. Theodore, who had stepped up in his crease a little to challenge the original shot, wasn't sure where the puck was, but he had a hunch. In an instant, as Guerin thought he was scoring the game-tying goal, Theodore spun around, sent his stick flying and blindly whipped his blocker hand behind him with his head turned the other way in a desperate move towards the goal line. Guerin's shot struck the blocker fractions of a second before it entered the net, and a star was born.

That save was played, and replayed, on every sports telecast in the hockey-playing world that night. Although the Canadiens went on to lose in the second round to the Carolina Hurricanes, the save vaulted Theodore into the upper stratosphere of hockey stardom. And it officially put an end to a rocky ascension where his ability to be a starting goalie in the NHL was constantly put into question.

That ascension essentially began when Theodore was born as the youngest of Ted and Marie-France Theodore's five sons in the Montréal suburb of Laval, Québec. When Jose was seven years old, his older brothers needed someone to play in nets. They put Jose into a set of goalie pads, and he hasn't taken them off since.

The beginning of Theodore's junior hockey career with the St-Jean Lynx of the Québec Major Junior Hockey League (QMJHL) was solid, but not spectacular in any sense. Although no one doubted that Theodore possessed talent, he wasn't seen to have any more talent than a number of other goaltending prospects from the Canadian Hockey League. At least that's what the Montréal Canadiens thought when they prepared their list for the 1994 draft.

The Canadiens had four goalies—Éric Fichaud, Jamie Storr, Dan Cloutier and Theodore—who they were happy to take with their second-round pick. As it turned out, the rest of the league made the decision easy for them because Theodore was the only one out of the four still available when the Canadiens selected him 44th overall.

For a kid who grew up in the suburbs of Montréal, it couldn't have turned out any better. "This has been my dream since I was young," Theodore said a week after the draft, "to play for or against the Canadiens."

Theodore led his new team, the Hull Olympiques, to the 1994–95 QMJHL championship and a berth in the Memorial Cup the following season before attending his first training camp with the Montréal Canadiens in 1995. Of course, Theodore had no illusions of making the team, and even if he did, they were instantly erased as soon as he saw Patrick Roy skating on the same ice as he was. The number one goalie's job with the Canadiens was secure, but at some point Roy had to retire. Roy was already verging on 30 during that training camp, and Theodore, at 19, looked to have the perfect timing. When Roy retires six or seven years down the road, Theodore would be primed to take his place.

Or so it seemed.

In December 1995, the foundations of the entire Canadiens franchise crumbled around them when Roy—after a very public stare-down with coach Mario Tremblay—vowed he would never play another game for Montréal. Canadiens general manager Réjean Houle didn't need long to find a taker for Roy's services, and within days of Roy's demand, he and Mike Keane were traded to the Colorado Avalanche.

In return, Houle got two wingers and a goaltender, Jocelyn Thibault. Thibault was only 20 years old and he already had two years of NHL experience behind him, which Theodore didn't. It appeared to everyone that Houle had just acquired the Canadiens goaltender of the future, the exact position Theodore thought he could fill.

"What can I do? I have no control over it. I'm not with the Canadiens, we'll see next season," Theodore said after the trade. "If I play well, everything will fall into place. If we play for the same team, we'll make a great duo. A goalie doesn't have to play 75 games a season. All I want to do is play in the NHL, preferably with Montréal. You never know what can happen."

Theodore apparently drew some inspiration from the trade and began playing the best hockey of his life. His numbers for Hull improved dramatically and earned him an invitation to join Canada's national junior team for the 1996 world championships. Although he platooned with Marc Denis throughout the early stages of the tournament, it was Theodore who got the call to start against the powerful Russians in the semi-final game.

Theodore rallied his overmatched Canadian teammates to a 4–3 victory with 46 saves, and he followed that up with a 33-save performance in Canada's 4–1 gold medal win over Sweden. He was named the tournament's, and thereby the world's, top goaltender.

"We're an emotional people and that spills over into our hockey," Theodore said in the jubilance of the Canadian dressing room. "We don't accept second place."

Theodore had a fantastic training camp with the Canadiens that September, allowing only two power play goals on 89 shots in two exhibition game victories. But Montréal felt it was unfair for Theodore to stay with the big club and sit on the bench behind Thibault, so he was sent to the Canadiens' American Hockey League (AHL) affiliate in Fredericton, New Brunswick, where he was the number one goalie.

When Thibault broke his finger in late October, Theodore was back in Montréal, and in the first NHL start of his career against the San Jose Sharks on November 2, 1996, he made 31 saves in a 4–3 over-time loss. The next night in Phoenix against the Coyotes, Theodore made a strong case for remain-ing with the big club with 46 saves in a 4–4 tie. "We can't send Theodore back down if he keeps play-ing like this," Tremblay said after the Phoenix game. "He's forcing our hand."

Theodore continued his strong play while Thibault recovered from his injury, so much so that Montréal decided to keep three goaltenders when Thibault was ready to return.

"I feel I'm good enough to play in the NHL," Theodore said once Tremblay announced he would stay in Montréal. "Two weeks ago, I wasn't sure because I didn't know what to expect...Every day, I feel I'm improving."

The bubble burst for Theodore less than a week later when he was sent back to the AHL after allowing three goals on 12 shots in a game against Florida. In Montréal, meanwhile, the locals were becoming restless with the tandem of Thibault and his backup Pat Jablonski as both of them faltered. In February, the Canadiens called Theodore back up from Fredericton and announced Jablonski was on the trade block.

Theodore played so well the rest of the year that many began to question whether he should be the starter instead of Thibault. But it was in the 1997 playoffs that Theodore made his mark on the notoriously fickle Montréal fans. The Canadiens were overmatched against the New Jersey Devils in the first round and it showed; Thibault allowed an average of five goals a game in three straight lopsided defeats. A desperate Tremblay called on Theodore to stop the bleeding, and he got the start at home in an effort to avoid a humiliating sweep. Theodore was up to the challenge, stopping 56 shots—including 28 after regulation time had ended—to lead Montréal to a 4–3 triple overtime win.

"I'll never forget it, that's for sure," Theodore said of his playoff debut. "Thirty years from now, I'll remember that game."

Theodore had to think he had proven his worth to the Canadiens brass. But that off-season, after the Devils beat Theodore and the Canadiens in game five, Montréal signed veteran goalie Andy Moog to share the load with Thibault. Before training camp had even begun, Theodore had practically no chance of making the team. Sure enough, near the end of training camp, Theodore was cut and sent to Fredericton.

He didn't play a single regular season game for Montréal in 1997–98, but for the second year in a row Theodore did finish the Canadiens final playoff game when he relieved Moog in Montréal's 3–1 loss to Buffalo in game four of the opening round. Moog retired that off-season, opening the door for Theodore to vie for a job in the NHL. This time, finally, he got his shot as the Canadiens went with a combination of him and Thibault. But both goalies played poorly to start the year, and the Canadiens lost their patience. Thibault was shipped off to the Chicago Blackhawks for veteran goalie Jeff Hackett, and Theodore was back in Fredericton by January.

Theodore and his agents, Bob Perno and Don Meehan, were beginning to lose patience with the Canadiens. "If we feel he has no future in Montréal," Perno said shortly after Theodore was demoted, "we'll do something over the summer."

It never got that far, as Theodore became the primary backup to Hackett in Montréal for the 1999–2000 season. Theodore played in 30 games while staying with Montréal the entire season for the first time since he was drafted five years earlier. His solid play led to the birth of a goaltending controversy in Montréal, as the media and fans wanted to see the hometown kid play more often.

They got what they wanted the following year when Hackett suffered a broken hand early in the season. This opened the door for Theodore, and he walked right through it, playing in a career-high 57 games, getting five shutouts and posting a 2.57 goals against average. But the highlight of the season came on January 3, 2001, in Long Island, New York.

The Canadiens had a 2–0 lead and the New York Islanders had pulled their goalie in the dying seconds of the game. The puck came behind the net, Theodore stopped it and sent a backhand skywards and down the ice. Although he was only attempting to clear his own zone while avoiding a potential penalty for shooting it out of play, Theodore's shot landed at centre ice and slowly meandered its way into the empty Islanders net.

"It was awesome," a beaming Theodore said after the game. "I was jumping all over the place. We got the win and the shutout, and I got a goal. It was a pretty good night for me."

Theodore became only the sixth goalie in NHL history to be credited for a goal, but in fact he was only the fourth goalie to actually shoot a puck into the net. The other two got credit for being the last player to touch a puck before an opponent put it in their own net.

Theodore solidified his status as the team's top goalie in 2000–01, winning the team's Molson Cup for the most three-star selections over the course of the season. But Hackett was still on the team come training camp, and the Canadiens wouldn't anoint either one of them as the starter because they both had great training camps.

But Hackett was 33 years old at this point, and he suffered an early-season injury for the second year in a row, this time a separated shoulder. Theodore was handed the reins. He played in 20 of the team's first 27 games in 2001–02 and was lights out, posting a 2.03 goals against average with a .931 save percentage over that time. "I've waited a long time for this, so I might as well take advantage," Theodore said then. "I'm at a young age. I'm only 25; to play this much is a bonus."

In January, as he was putting the finishing touches on his fourth shutout of the season in a 2–0 win over the Washington Capitals, Theodore was named to his first NHL all-star team. It was at around the same time that Canadiens head coach Michel Therrien announced that even though Hackett was healthy enough to play, Theodore was his number one for the rest of the season.

With 19 games left in the regular season, Hackett suffered an injury to the same shoulder, ending his campaign. The pressure now fell on Theodore to lead the team to the playoffs for the first time in four years, the Canadiens' longest playoff drought ever.

"Jose has to find a way for our team to get to the playoffs, nothing else will be accepted after three years [out of the playoffs]," Canadiens goaltending coach Roland Melanson said bluntly. "Jose might play every game, a lot is riding on his shoulders."

Theodore did everything that was asked of him, and more. He played in 21 of the Canadiens' last

22 games, including 17 in a row that culminated in a seven-game winning streak to clinch a Canadiens playoff berth. The Canadiens met the Bruins in the first round as huge underdogs, but Theodore proved to be the equalizer. Although he struggled through the first four games of the series, his Canadiens teammates picked him up by scoring enough goals to earn a 2–2 split. That's when Theodore took over, stopping 43 shots in Boston to hand the Canadiens a 2–1 win, even though they were out-shot 44–13. Then came game six, and Theodore's miraculous blocker save on Bill Guerin that pre-served the Canadiens' series victory.

After the Canadiens were eliminated by the Carolina Hurricanes, Theodore's summer of love began. He had already earned the Roger Crozier Saving Grace Award for posting the league's best save percentage at .931, but at the 2002 NHL awards that summer Theodore cleaned up. He beat out his boyhood idol Patrick Roy to win the Vezina Trophy as the league's top goalie, and then, with the final award of the night, Wayne Gretzky announced Theodore as the recipient of the Hart Trophy for the league's MVP.

"My legs are weak," an astounded Theodore said after the ceremony. "I couldn't believe it when Gretzky pronounced my name. I still can't believe it."

Theodore's instant stardom was a little difficult for him to handle. That summer, he accepted

nearly every invitation sent to him, filming com-
mercials and playing in a rock concert with Québec
star Éric Lapointe. He was also embroiled in a summer of contract negotiations with the Canadiens
that stretched into September. Theodore finally
agreed to a three-year deal that paid him $5.5 mil-
lion a year, making him the highest-paid Canadiens'
player in the team's storied history.

The summer whirlwind was a little too much.
Theodore was not properly prepared for the
2002–03 season, and his play suffered as a result.
The Canadiens missed the playoffs again, largely
because Theodore's numbers had ballooned into
the realm of mediocrity. "I never had the time to
clear my head," Theodore said after the 2002–03
season was over. "Our [2001–02] season ended
May 15, I got the [Hart and Vezina] trophies on
June 20 and a wave of events followed. Even my
parents were complaining that they never got to
see me. When camp began, I still wasn't hungry
to strap on the pads. It felt like camp came quickly."

Theodore kept a lower profile in the summer of
2003, due largely to the arrests of his father and
brothers in connection with a loan-sharking ring
operating out of the Montréal Casino. There were
also published photos of Theodore hanging out
with members of the criminal biker gang the Hells
Angels. Although police made it clear Theodore
was not a target of their loan-sharking investiga-
tion and that the photos proved nothing, some
people in Montréal began to wonder if it might be

a good idea to trade him. It was a good thing for the Canadiens that they didn't.

Theodore reverted to his Hart Trophy form in 2003–04, posting a 33–28 record with a 2.18 goals against average and .919 save percentage to lead the Canadiens back to the playoffs to once again meet, and beat, the Boston Bruins in the first round of the playoffs. But Theodore, even after his dream season in 2002, and even though he has achieved star status in the NHL, will never be satisfied.

"I wasn't happy just to be drafted," Theodore once said. "I wanted to be a starter, I wanted to go to the All-Star game. I haven't won the Stanley Cup yet, so it's important to aim high, and you have to be ready to make the sacrifices to achieve your goals because it doesn't happen by chance. You create your own luck, and your own destiny."

He's created himself a pretty good destiny in Montréal.

One Shot, One Goal

Although Jose Theodore has proved to be one of the best goaltenders in the NHL, his career didn't get off to such a rollicking start. On February 21, 1996, in Hartford, Connecticut, Canadiens goalie Pat Jablonski had been shelled in nets, and a nervous 19-year-old Theodore was sent in to finish the game.

"I remember it wasn't a good start," Theodore said. "On my first shot, Sami Kapanen scored on a 2-on-1. But at least it was a nice goal, and not one from centre ice."

Chapter Nine

Vincent Lecavalier and Brad Richards

V incent Lecavalier is a large man, so it stands to reason that he casts a pretty imposing shadow. Just ask Brad Richards, the man who has lived in that shadow most of his hockey-playing life. The Tampa Bay Lightning forwards—born only 11 days apart in 1980—have been joined at the hip ever since they were 14 years old. They played at the same high school in Saskatchewan, the same major junior team in Québec and the same team in the pros.

But long before the two became NHL stars and Stanley Cup champions, it was always Lecavalier who attracted all the scouts, all the attention, all the praise, and nearly all the credit for anything Richards did. Lecavalier was ordained as the best forward to come out of Québec since Mario Lemieux and as the "Michael Jordan of hockey" by Tampa Bay Lightning owner Arthur Williams after the Lightning took Lecavalier with the first overall pick in the 1998 draft.

Basically, Lecavalier was expected to duplicate the exploits of two of the biggest superstars in sports, and he was barely 18 years old. But if Lecavalier was the chosen one, Richards was the overlooked one. Even though he always put up numbers similar to Lecavalier's as they were made their way through bantam, midget and finally major junior hockey, Richards was constantly being slighted because he did not possess his good buddy's impressive stature. But by the spring of 2004, just before the Lightning made a run at the Stanley Cup, Richards and Lecavalier had each gone to the opposite ends of the spectrum.

Richards was the consistent offensive producer who never failed to reach 60 points in his four years with the Lightning, a pleasant surprise for a third-round NHL draft pick. On the other end there was Lecavalier, the franchise's supposed saviour whose six-year career to that point had been marked by inconsistent play, feuding with coaches, unmet expectations and having his team captaincy removed. All of a sudden, Richards was the proven commodity and Lecavalier the one with something to prove. But the playoffs finished with Lecavalier putting to rest any doubts about his character, and Richards officially entering the brotherhood of NHL stars.

It was exactly how Lecavalier and Richards dreamed it would turn out when they were 14 years old and bunked next to each other at Athol Murray College of Notre Dame in tiny Wilcox, Saskatchewan. The boys were both intimidated by being so far away from home at such a young age and took an instant liking to each other.

Lecavalier, who came from the Montréal suburb of Île Bizard, was the youngest of Yves and Christiane Lecavalier's three children. Yves, a firefighter and former junior hockey player, took his son to the rink when he was only two and a half years old. Lecavalier played organized hockey at the age of four against kids twice his age, and by the time he was six years old, locals were already coming to the rink just to watch him play.

Lecavalier's older brother Philippe had attended Notre Dame and had a full hockey scholarship to play defence at Clarkson University in Potsdam, New York. When the younger Lecavalier left home to play at Notre Dame, he hoped to follow the path his brother marked for him.

Richards came to Saskatchewan from the tiny fishing hamlet of Murray Harbor, Prince Edward Island, and was the eldest child of Glen and Delite Richards. Richards' father was a lobster fisherman, like his grandfather and great-grandfather were. Similar to Lecavalier, Richards was first taken out on the ice by his father when he was two and a half years old. Although Richards had all the respect in the world for the difficult work his parents endured in order to put food on the table, lobster fishing wasn't something he wanted to do for a living.

"I guess if I wasn't playing hockey, I'd be fishing and playing hockey in the senior league back home," Richards said during the 2003–04 playoffs. "I just didn't want to get up every morning and go fishing with my mom and dad. My brother likes it, but I couldn't do it. I had to be a hockey player, because I wasn't going to be a fisherman."

Richards and his family decided the best way to do that was to go to Saskatchewan and Notre Dame, where he would have a chance to play a higher calibre of hockey than what he was exposed to in tiny Prince Edward Island. The coach at Notre Dame at the time, Terry O'Malley, knew he had a stud in Lecavalier, but he wasn't positive Richards could overcome being only 5-foot-6 as a 14-year-old. "Lecavalier was tall, even then, and Richards was a lot shorter," O'Malley recalled. "Lecavalier was an obvious shoo-in to make our top bantam team, but Richards went down to the wire."

Richards' uncanny knack for making things happen offensively with his superior ice vision and passing skills eventually won over the coaches at Notre Dame, and the pair were the only grade nine students to play on the school's top bantam team in 1994–95.

The following year the good buddies dominated the bantam league, with Lecavalier notching 104 points and Richards getting 99 points. Both were invited to join the Notre Dame midget team for their playoff run and finished one-two in post-season scoring.

Even though Lecavalier had come to Saskatchewan with hopes of getting a college scholarship, he couldn't resist the lure of junior hockey after the Rimouski Océanic of the Québec Major Junior Hockey League (QMJHL) selected him with the fourth overall pick in the 1996 midget draft.

Richards, however, was looked over in the QMJHL draft and stayed behind at Notre Dame for another year of seasoning. He played for the Notre Dame Junior A team in 1996–97 despite only being the age of a first-year midget player.

Lecavalier's arrival in Rimouski, meanwhile, took the QMJHL by storm. It didn't take long for the Québec media to compare him to other great French-Canadian stars, and by the end of the year he was widely considered the province's best hockey prospect since Lemieux was shattering the league's scoring records.

Before the 1997 QMJHL draft, Lecavalier encouraged his bosses in Rimouski to go have a look at Richards, who was on his way to scoring 87 points and being named the Saskatchewan Junior Hockey League's rookie of the year. The Rimouski scouts were sold, and the Océanic used their first-round pick in the draft to reunite the friends. Richards adapted to the major junior level remarkably well, tying Lecavalier for the team-scoring lead with

115 points in 1997–98 and being named a QMJHL all-star.

But, once again, it was Lecavalier who drew all the attention, being named to the Canadian national team while Richards watched the world junior tournament at home. Lecavalier was the consensus number one prospect for the 1998 NHL entry draft, and Richards, it was believed by some, was simply riding the coat tails of his talented friend and linemate, reaping the benefits of playing with such a can't-miss prospect.

After Lecavalier went, as everyone expected, number one to Tampa Bay at the 1998 draft, he began talking up his friend to the Lightning staff, who didn't pick again until the third round, 64 picks away. Richards was still available when the 65th pick came up, and the Lightning grabbed him. Once Richards was through getting his jersey at the podium and doing his interviews, Lecavalier was waiting to greet him.

"I can't get rid of him," Richards joked to a reporter after the draft.

The Lightning said his relationship with Lecavalier was a factor in their decision to pick Richards, but it wasn't the only factor. "I'd be lying if I didn't tell you it helped that they've been together and they're friends," Lightning head scout Don Murdoch said after the draft. "But we didn't just take him because he's [Lecavalier's] linemate. We took

Brad Richards because Brad Richards is a heck of a hockey player."

He just wasn't as good of a hockey player as Lecavalier, not then anyway. At training camp, Richards was hardly given a sniff before being shipped back to Rimouski, but Lecavalier was instantly installed as a centrepiece of the Lightning attack at the ripe age of 18.

With Lecavalier being fed to the NHL wolves in Tampa Bay, Richards became the undisputed leader of the Océanic in Rimouski. He piled up 131 points and passed Lecavalier to become Rimouski's all-time leading scorer (though he was passed six years later by another kid from the Maritimes, Sidney Crosby), but he still wasn't invited by Canada to play for the national junior team. "I've been having the best season of my life," said the 18-year-old Richards upon hearing news of the snub. "But it's a 19-year-old tournament and that's the way it is."

That wasn't the end of Richards' disappointment. At Lightning training camp before the 1999–2000 season, he was determined to earn a spot on the team and join Lecavalier, who had a decent rookie season the year before with 13 goals and 15 assists while playing on the third line and in all 82 games. But Richards didn't stick and went back to Rimouski for his third season of major junior while Lecavalier prepared for his second year in the NHL.

It was the widest gap in the two friends' careers since they met, and it was also the best years either of them had ever had. Lecavalier led the team in goals with 25 and in assists with 42, living up to all the hype that had surrounded him a year earlier. On March 11, 2000, Lightning head coach Steve Ludzik, following the trade of team captain Chris Gratton, named Lecavalier to take his place. He became the youngest full-time captain in NHL history at 19 years of age, two years younger than his hockey idol Steve Yzerman was when he was named captain of the Detroit Red Wings.

Tampa Bay general manager Rick Dudley saw nothing wrong with thrusting a teenager into such an important leadership role, largely because he had the support of his teammates. "He sets the example," Dudley said of the decision. "He's not loud, but he has a presence. The day we traded Gratton, 10 players called me to say they wanted Vinny as captain."

One of those players who supported the decision was goaltender Dan Cloutier, who remembered a time he was feeling down after a couple of bad games while sitting next to Lecavalier on the plane. "He started telling me about how things were going to get better, and he suggested a couple of things to turn my game around," Cloutier remembered. "It was weird. He's a 19-year-old kid, right? But the way Vinny carries himself, it's as if he's been in the league 10 years."

Richards, meanwhile, was doing everything in his power to prove to the Lightning that they made a mistake cutting him. He led all Canadian Hockey

League (CHL) scorers with 71 goals and 115 assists for Rimouski in 1999–2000, posting the highest point total in the QMJHL in 11 years. He also had a ridiculous plus/minus rating of plus-80, by far the best in the country.

Richards was finally selected to represent Canada at the 2000 world junior championships, posting 6 points in seven games for the bronze-medal winning squad. But it was in the playoffs that Richards showed everyone what he could do with a puck. He scored 37 points in only 12 games as Rimouski romped its way to the 2000 QMJHL title to earn a berth in the Memorial Cup in Halifax.

A few days before Rimouski played in the tournament final, Dudley told reporters in Tampa that he felt it was unlikely the Lightning would sign Richards before the June 1 deadline, at which point he could re-enter the NHL draft as the CHL player of the year and scoring leader. "He's a kid we'd love to have," Dudley said at the time, "but if it doesn't work out, it's not the end of the world for the Tampa Bay Lightning."

Lecavalier was aware of his friend's predicament, and called Richards for a little pep talk. "He told me to keep believing I was the best player on the ice," Richards said, "not to let the contract talk get to me."

Richards was having a pretty mediocre tournament—only by his lofty standards—leading into the Memorial Cup final with 6 points in three games. As the Barrie Colts prepared to face Rimouski in the final, Colts forward Mike Jefferson (who later changed his name to Mike Danton) told reporters that Richards "wouldn't last five games" in the rougher Ontario Hockey League.

Richards responded with actions rather than words as he got 2 goals and 2 assists to lead Rimouski to a 6–2 win in the final for the first Memorial Cup championship in franchise history. Richards, just after being crowned the tournament's MVP, couldn't help but gloat a little over Jefferson's comments, especially after he refused to shake Richards' hand after the game.

"What can he say?" Richards asked after the game. "We won 6–2, I had a great game and we won the Memorial Cup. There's nothing he can say."

Richards, all of a sudden and just a few days before the deadline, found himself with a lot of leverage in his contract negotiations with Dudley. Fearing he would lose the top player in Canadian junior hockey, Dudley agreed to Richards' demand that he receive the maximum salary allowable to a rookie, signing him to a three-year contract laden with bonus clauses.

"I haven't slept a whole lot lately and I'm unbelievably happy to get this done," Richards said after signing on the dotted line.

The following fall, there was no way Tampa Bay could justify cutting Richards from the 2000–01 team, and he was once again on the same team with Lecavalier. Richards thrived almost immediately, being named the NHL's rookie of the month for October and finishing with 62 points in 82 games to come second in the Calder Trophy voting for rookie of the year.

But that season was the beginning of Lecavalier's fall from grace. Halfway through the year, Lightning coach Ludzik was replaced by John Tortorella, a brash disciplinarian from Boston. Tortorella and Lecavalier clashed almost immediately. The following season, Tortorella stripped Lecavalier of his captaincy and asked Dudley if it was possible to trade Lecavalier, who he called "Lazy Vinny."

Dudley began accepting offers for his disgruntled centre, but it was Dudley who was shown the door by upper Lightning management. Incoming general manager Jay Feaster immediately went about repairing the damage done, assuring Lecavalier he was still important to the franchise. "I told Vincent, straight up, I would not be the answer to the trivia question, 'Which stupid general manager traded Vincent Lecavalier?'" Feaster said.

It was a good thing for the Lightning that Feaster felt that way, because Lecavalier soon combined with Richards to lead the franchise to the NHL promised land. Lecavalier had a career-best 78 points in 2002–03 while Richards had his best season with 74 points. But it was in the 2003–04 playoffs that the two really shone.

Richards had outscored Lecavalier during the regular season with yet another career-high of

79 points to Lecavalier's 66. He had become, in the eyes of many observers, the Lightning's most reliable performer and brightest young star at the age of 24, supplanting Lecavalier in that role after years of comparisons and slights.

When the playoffs hit, Richards continued his incredible season, but this time it was Lecavalier who was out to prove his doubters wrong. The Lightning beat the New York Islanders in five games in round one, but Lecavalier failed to register so much as a point. In round two, Tampa Bay was to face Lecavalier's hometown Montréal Canadiens, and that's when the kid from Île Bizard came into his own. With just 17 seconds to play in game three, Lecavalier somehow managed to put his stick between his legs to tip a shot into the Montréal net for the game-tying goal, which was then followed by Richards' goal just over a minute into overtime. The Lightning won and gained a 3–0 stranglehold in a series they went on to sweep.

During the series, the chemistry in the Lightning dressing room was nearly derailed when Hockey Canada announced its team for the upcoming World Cup of Hockey. The Lightning's and the league's leading scorer, Martin St-Louis, was obviously named to the team, but so was Richards, finally giving him the validation as being one of the best players in hockey, something that he had sought for so long. Except that Richards couldn't be as happy as he wanted because, for the first time in his life, he had beaten out Lecavalier for a spot on the team. Shortly after the Canadian team was announced, the two went out for brunch.

"Brad didn't want to bring it up because he had been named and I hadn't and it was not talked about until I brought it up," Lecavalier said. "Finally I congratulated him on making the team and he said 'You should have been there too.' Of course I thought so too. I was upset. I admit it but I kept it to myself."

Lecavalier used the slight as motivation and revealed a side of his game no one had ever seen. Although Tampa beat the Flyers in seven games to advance to the Stanley Cup final, the only reason Philadelphia was even in that position was thanks to the bruising play of centre Keith Primeau, and his physical style rubbed off on Lecavalier. In the final series against the Calgary Flames, Lecavalier was seeking out people to hit and, in game three of the Cup finals, went toe-to-toe with Flames power forward Jarome Iginla in one of the most memorable fights in finals history.

"I've been trying to play more physical in the last five or six games," said Lecavalier during the Cup series. "I saw what [Keith] Primeau did [for Philadelphia] in our last series and how he was hitting everybody and I tried to do some of that. It gets you in the game."

Lecavalier's improved aggressiveness, and an NHL record of seven game-winning goals in the playoffs from Richards, led the Lightning to the Stanley Cup, beating Calgary in seven games with Richards awarded the Conn Smythe Trophy as playoff MVP.

Shortly after the playoffs, Hockey Canada was informed that Yzerman was unable to play in the World Cup. Team Canada executive director Wayne Gretzky immediately called Lecavalier to take his hero's place. There was no doubt who would be the first person Lecavalier called as soon as he hung up the phone with Gretzky. "I called Brad right after," Lecavalier told reporters after his selection. "He was really happy. We've been great friends for so long and we've been through so much together."

While Richards got his shot at redemption in the NHL playoffs, fulfilling a lifelong dream to bring the Stanley Cup back to his sleepy fishing village of Murray Harbor, Lecavalier breathed new life into his career and solidified his status as one of the world's best players in the World Cup. He scored 2 goals, including the dramatic game-winner in overtime of the semi-final against the Czech Republic, and added 5 assists to be named World Cup MVP after Canada downed Finland 3–2 in the tournament final.

The performance put forth by Richards and Lecavalier over the previous six months completed the coronation of the NHL's newest one-two punch, one that should be feared by every team in the league for the next decade.

~∞~

Chapter Ten

Jay Bouwmeester

The seasoned hockey scout walked into the arena completely unprepared for what he was about to see, probably because he had never seen anything like it. Barry Trapp had come to watch the Alberta under-17 team's camp in Calgary, conveniently close to Trapp's office at Hockey Canada where he was the director of scouting. When Trapp looked out on the ice, his eye was immediately drawn to a man-sized defenceman with a buttery stride effortlessly skating faster than the best 17-year-old players in the province.

Trapp's natural conclusion was that this was an older player, someone just coming out for a skate, maybe even needing some work coming back from an injury. But he had to make sure. So he walked over to a group of scouts who had been watching the proceedings on the ice to look for an answer.

"Who's the major junior guy out there skating with the kids?" Trapp asked them.

"That's 14-year-old Jay Bouwmeester," one of
the scouts replied.

Trapp was stunned. "I sat down and watched him
the entire hour and a half," Trapp recalled years
after that first encounter. "I was mesmerized."

Any time Jay Bouwmeester put on a pair of
skates, he tended to have this similar effect on anyone who happened to be watching him. Throughout his childhood dominating the Alberta minor
hockey ranks, right up to his growing role with the
NHL's Florida Panthers, Bouwmeester's fluid skating stride has led hockey people to extend the
boundaries of hyperbole.

"This boy glides better than most people skate,"
Columbus Blue Jackets general manager Doug
MacLean once said after watching a 16-year-old
Bouwmeester become the youngest player to play
for Canada at the world junior hockey champi-
onships in 2000.

The general manager of the Tampa Bay Lightning
at the time, Rick Dudley, took it one step farther
after watching Bouwmeester at the same tournament. "He's got size, poise and he skates as fast
backwards as most guys do forwards," he noted.

Bouwmeester was born to skate. A tried cliché,
perhaps, but in this case it couldn't describe the situation any better. He had begun walking when he
was just nine months old, so Bouwmeester was
quicker than most kids to look for new challenges.

When he was one and a half years old, his mother Gena went downstairs to find that her infant son had somehow managed to get his older sister Jill's roller skates on and was going for a leisurely skate in the basement.

Not too long after that, when Bouwmeester was about three, his father Dan—who played defence for the University of Alberta hockey team from 1968–72—decided it was time for his son to try the real thing. Every winter, Dan flooded the backyard of the family's Edmonton home to encourage his kids to skate. But Bouwmeester didn't need any encouragement.

"I'll always remember the first time I put him on skates," his father recalled. "I was holding on to him and it was just, 'Get away from me Dad! I want to go on my own.' That was from day one."

But that was as close to a hockey rink as Bouwmeester would get for the next three years, as his father wanted him to perfect his skating before playing in organized games. "The better you skate backward," his father told him as he made his way around the backyard, "the better you skate forward."

Bouwmeester was instantly hooked, spending every available winter moment in the backyard mastering the powerful stride that would one day have NHL scouts drooling. But his natural athletic ability did not only apply to hockey. He was a skilled basketball and volleyball player as well as an eight-handicap golfer by the time he was 14. He also excelled in track and field, once claiming the city long jump championship. But hockey always came first, and Bouwmeester was determined to become the best.

"A lot of kids don't have Jay's work ethic," Dan said. "I never had to push him. Since he was very little, he had a stick in his hand. He was bashing a ball around from the time he could pick it up."

Bouwmeester began playing organized hockey at age six, and by the time he was nine he was already well known in Edmonton hockey circles for his skating ability. His father was his coach every year until he turned 14, by which point Bouwmeester was the best minor hockey defenceman in Alberta. He was already 6-foot-2 when he completed his first year of bantam with 13 goals and 36 assists in 35 games to be named the Alberta Bantam Hockey Association's most outstanding defenceman and rookie of the year.

Bouwmeester was a no-brainer top choice for the Medicine Hat Tigers in the Western Hockey League's (WHL) 1997 bantam draft, and a year later he played in the Tigers' last eight games of the season as a 15-year-old, scoring two goals and adding an assist. His official arrival to the major junior ranks in 1999–2000 was met with huge anticipation. Bouwmeester, now 6-foot-4 and 200 pounds at 16 years of age, was instantly one of the top defencemen, not only for the Tigers, but in all of Canadian junior hockey.

Trapp never forgot watching Bouwmeester two years earlier at the under-17 camp in Calgary. So when it came time to send out the invitations to the 2000 Canadian junior team's selection camp in December, Bouwmeester's name was on the mailing list.

"It's a big honour for me to get an invite," Bouwmeester said after hearing the big news. "I can't remember how long I've been watching the tournament. Every Christmas we would watch the world junior tournament."

Bouwmeester was one of two 16-year-olds invited to the camp in Kitchener, Ontario, that year, joining Mississauga Ice Dogs centre Jason Spezza. It was the first time Hockey Canada had invited two 16-year-olds to try out for the national junior team, which is usually composed of 18- and 19-year-old players. The unprecedented move made for a media frenzy surrounding the two phenoms. "At the world junior training camp in Kitchener there was a huge media gathering," Trapp recalled. "[Bouwmeester] took one spin around the ice, and you could hear a pin drop in that arena."

While Spezza appeared at ease handling the mass of reporters covering the camp, Bouwmeester wasn't. Many words have been used to describe Bouwmeester, but no one ever accused him of being chatty. Shy, mild-mannered, soft-spoken, reserved, demure and just plain quiet are far better terms to describe Bouwmeester's demeanor.

"When you're with Jay, it's like you've got your own room on the road," Bouwmeester's future roommate with the Florida Panthers, Lance Ward, said during his rookie season in the NHL. "I look over and I'm not sure he's breathing. He doesn't snore. He sits so still. The kid is so quiet, he tiptoes to the bathroom at night."

Dealing with the new distractions probably contributed to Bouwmeester getting off to a slow start at the selection camp, and it didn't help that he was uncomfortable wearing the full face cage that is mandatory for 16 year olds at the international level. "I know he doesn't like it," Dan Bouwmeester said during the camp. "I told Jay, 'Tell them you'll wear a tutu if it will help you get on the team.'"

When it came time to make the cuts, Bouwmeester had played his way into a good position to make the team without having to make like a ballerina. The Canadian junior team's tradition was to inform the players who had been cut with a phone call at the crack of dawn. "I went to bed and just hoped I wouldn't get woken by a ringing," Bouwmeester said. "When I opened my eyes and it was morning, I was about happy as I can be."

With Bouwmeester and Spezza both being selected to play for Canada, they joined Wayne Gretzky and Eric Lindros as the only 16-year-olds to make the cut. Bouwmeester, at 16 years and three months, became the youngest player to suit up for

Canada when he took to the ice for the world junior championships in Sweden.

Bouwmeester saw limited minutes when the tournament began, but by the end he was in the team's four-man rotation on defence, and his play had left a major impression on NHL types in attendance. He finished his first full season of major junior with 13 goals and 21 assists in 64 games, and in 2001 he was one of Canada's top defencemen at the world juniors despite still being the youngest player on the team.

"He's like ready-mix cake, just add water," said Brian Burke, general manager of the Vancouver Canucks at the time, while watching the 2001 tournament in Moscow. "The only question I have for him is what [jersey] number he would want."

While Bouwmeester was away in Moscow, Bob Loucks took over as the head coach in Medicine Hat. Although Loucks had heard nothing but good things about his top defenceman, he remained somewhat skeptical that Bouwmeester was indeed as good as people said he was. His doubts were very quickly put to rest. "Everybody was telling me how good he was but I couldn't quite believe that, nobody is that good," Loucks said. "The very first time I saw him step on the ice, well, he took two or three strides and I was giggling. He's that good, and you see it that quick."

Just days after his 18th birthday early in the 2001–02 season, Bouwmeester was named the top prospect for the 2002 NHL entry draft by Red Line Report, a status he would never relinquish. Bouwmeester was almost single-handedly responsible for the Tigers defence in 2001–02, sometimes logging up to 35 minutes of ice time for a losing team that missed the WHL playoffs for a third year in a row. He was also counted upon to anchor the Canadian junior team's defensive corps in 2002, his third year on the national squad.

After two straight bronze medals at the tournament, the Canadians finally reached the final against Russia but lost 5–4. Bouwmeester was at his dominant best, however, leading the tournament in plus/minus rating and being named a first team all-star, though the accolades did nothing to quell the sting of losing what was probably his last shot at world junior gold. "This is really disappointing because the game was just so close," Bouwmeester said after returning home. "But over the years, it will become something we can be proud of."

Bouwmeester finished his year for Medicine Hat with 11 goals and 50 assists in 61 games to earn a spot on the WHL's 2001–02 first all-star team. His coach Loucks knew that was the last time he would see Bouwmeester in a Tigers uniform. "I'd give up two of my own kids to have him back," Loucks had said, only half joking. "Jay will be one of the best NHL defensemen of all time."

By the time the 2002 NHL draft rolled around in June, it became obvious to most observers that

Bouwmeester would go first overall to the Florida Panthers.

"We have guys on our staff who have been scouting for 17 years, and he's probably the best skating defenseman any of us have ever seen," Panthers director of scouting Tim Murray said. "He's special. It's so rare that a guy that size is so agile and has such great speed."

But Dudley, who had been hired by the Panthers a month before the draft to be their general manager, played coy when reporters asked him if he was selecting Bouwmeester with the first pick. This act made MacLean, whose Columbus Blue Jackets had the third pick, very nervous. MacLean coveted London Knights winger Rick Nash, and while he was pretty sure Florida would take Bouwmeester, he didn't want to run the risk of losing Nash to either the Panthers or the Atlanta Thrashers, who had the second pick.

As Bouwmeester sat with his family in the stands of the Air Canada Centre in Toronto, completely prepared to be the first pick as everyone was telling him he would be, MacLean made a bold move just minutes before the draft began. MacLean offered Dudley the Blue Jackets' pick at number three, and the option to switch picks with Columbus in the 2003 draft in exchange for the first pick. Dudley, after sending a couple of late-round picks to Atlanta to make sure they didn't pick Bouwmeester, seized the opportunity to improve his club's draft status for the following year and pulled the trigger on the deal.

When it was Florida's time to pick third, Bouwmeester was still sitting in the stands, and Dudley got the guy he wanted all along. Although everyone assumed Bouwmeester would feel cheated out of a once-in-a-lifetime chance to be the first pick in the draft, the cool-headed defenceman insisted he couldn't care less. "I wound up with the team I thought I was going to anyway," he said after the draft. "It doesn't matter if you're number one or number three...a few years down the road, nobody remembers who went where."

The Panthers, a rebuilding team with very little established talent, inserted Bouwmeester straight into their top-four defensive rotation after his first NHL training camp showed that he could handle the jump from junior hockey to the pro ranks.

"I'd say he looks a lot closer to a four-year NHLer than a raw rookie," Dudley said before Bouwmeester's first regular season NHL game. "He's done wonderfully well so far. He's shown absolutely no intimidation at all. He makes the same crisp passes, still has the same vision and the wonderful feet he showed in junior."

On October 7, 2002, just 10 days after his 19th birthday, Bouwmeester signed a three-year contract with incentive clauses that could make it worth up to $11 million. He was worth the investment, playing over 20 minutes a night on the

Panthers' second defence pairing and taking part in all 82 of Florida's games as a rookie.

"The skating, that's what everybody obviously talks about because it's so wonderful," Dudley said. "But it's his vision and his thinking; that to me separates him from any other rookie. He sees the ice as well as any player on our team. His vacating of the zone is certainly, in my opinion, the best on our team already."

Although his transition to NHL life on the ice was a smooth one, adapting to life off the ice was a little rougher on Bouwmeester. It was the first time he had ever lived alone, and there were certain things he couldn't handle. For instance, when the Panthers rookies took the rest of the team out for dinner, a standard initiation ritual for first-year players, Bouwmeester brought enough cash to cover his portion of the $4000 tab. No credit cards or bank accounts for this rookie.

"He had trouble getting a social security number down here for a long time, so he couldn't get a bank account," said Ward, his roommate on the road. "He had three paycheques in his hotel room. I'm sure if he'd gone in to see the bank manager he could have got one, but he didn't want to bother him, I guess."

Although Bouwmeester was chosen to play in the 2002–03 YoungStars game during all-star weekend, he wasn't considered for rookie of the year honours largely because of his minus-29 defensive rating. The statistic is somewhat unfair in that it doesn't take into account that the Panthers often put Bouwmeester on the ice against the opposition's best forwards.

His play that season was good enough to persuade Hockey Canada to invite him to play on the senior men's team at the 2003 world championships, where he was once again the youngest player on the team. The 20-year-old Bouwmeester was a rock on the Canadian blue line, and he helped lead the team to its first world championship victory in six years.

As Bouwmeester stood on the blue line basking in his first championship victory, he heard the public address announcer call his name. Although he wasn't sure why he was doing it, Bouwmeester skated to centre ice and accepted a glass vase. It was only when he returned to join his teammates on the blue line that they told him he had been selected as the tournament's top defenceman.

His confidence strengthened by the world championships, Bouwmeester had an even better season on the Panthers blue line in 2003–04. He was second on the team in ice time, with over 23 minutes a game, and improved on his previous year's point total with 20 despite missing 18 games with a broken foot.

Bouwmeester returned to the world championships after that season and scored the game-winning goal in the gold medal final against

Sweden as Canada won consecutive championships for the first time since 1959. His strong play at the 2004 championships and his obvious potential as one of the burgeoning stars of the NHL got Bouwmeester a spot on Canada's team for the World Cup of Hockey, a best-on-best tournament where every NHL player was available to represent his country.

He inherited the spot of St. Louis Blues stalwart Chris Pronger, to whom Bouwmeester was most often compared, but it was clear that the youngster was only there as a spare part in case one of the team's top-six were to succumb to an injury. When Ed Jovanovski and Wade Redden were both injured in Canada's first two games, Bouwmeester stepped in and had an extraordinary tournament, not looking the least bit out of place among the best hockey players in the world as Canada went undefeated to win the World Cup.

Although everybody who had ever seen him play predicted Bouwmeester would be this good, no one could have predicted it would happen so soon. At the ripe age of 20, Bouwmeester was atop the hockey world, and he has no intention of coming down any time soon.

Finding Inspiration

Even though Jay Bouwmeester grew up in Edmonton, he was never a part of Oiler nation. Born in 1983, Bouwmeester has no memories of watching Wayne Gretzky feeding Jari Kurri for yet another goal, Grant Fuhr stoning someone on a breakaway, or Glen Sather chewing gum at a feverish pace behind the Oilers bench. Paul Coffey, the player whose skating stride Bouwmeester was constantly said to have copied, was out of Edmonton by the time Bouwmeester was three years old.

So where did he look for his hockey inspiration? To Michigan, where another quiet leader plied his trade in unassuming fashion: Steve Yzerman.

"He's my favourite player and always has been," Bouwmeester said. "I always liked the way he worked and played the game both ways."

As far as role models go, Bouwmeester could have done far worse.

NOTES ON SOURCES

Literally thousands of newspaper and magazine articles were used to shape the material found in this book. But those articles would simply be blank pages if it weren't for the dedicated work of NHL beat reporters across Canada and the United States who provided daily accounts of the players profiled here.

With youth being the common element in each of these players, there are very few books that have been written about most of them. One of the few, Jeff Rud's *Hockey's Young Superstars: The 25 Hottest Players on Ice* published by Raincoast Books (Vancouver, 2003), was a valuable source of background facts.

But most of the information and quotes came courtesy of the following news outlets and publications: *Atlanta Journal-Constitution, Associated Press, Boston Globe, Boston Herald, Calgary Herald, Calgary Sun, Canadian Press, Canwest News Service, The* (Wisconsin) *Capital Times, The* (Charlottetown) *Guardian, The* (Chatham) *Daily News, Chicago Tribune, Columbus Dispatch, Dallas Morning News, Edmonton Journal, Edmonton Sun, Financial Post, Globe and Mail, Halifax Daily News, Halifax Chronicle Herald,* Hockeydb.com, *Hockey Digest, The Hockey News, Le Journal de Montréal, The* (Kamloops) *Daily News, Kingston Whig-Standard, Knight-Ridder Newspapers, Miami Herald, Minneapolis Star Tribune, The* (Montréal) *Gazette, National Hockey League Official Guide & Record Book,*

National Post, The (New Glasgow) *Evening News, New York Daily News,* (New York) *Newsday, New York Times,* NHL.com, NHLPA.com, *Ottawa Citizen, Ottawa Sun, Palm Beach Post, Philadelphia Daily News, Philadelphia Inquirer, Portland* (Maine) *Press Herald, La Presse, Regina Leader-Post, Rocky Mountain News, St. Louis Post-Dispatch, The* (Saskatoon) *StarPhoenix, The Sault Star, South Florida Sun-Sentinel, Southam News, The Sporting News, Sports Illustrated, The* (Summerside) *Journal Pioneer, Tampa Tribune, Toronto Star, Toronto Sun, Transcontinental Media, The* (Truro) *Daily News,* TSN.ca, *TSN Magazine, The* (Vancouver) *Province, Vancouver Sun, Washington Post, Windsor Star, Winnipeg Free Press, Wisconsin State Journal.*

ARPON BASU

Since he was eight years old, Arpon had been telling people he would one day make the National Hockey League. Any chance of that happening as a player, however, came to a crashing halt when, at age 15, Basu realized to his horror that he was completely devoid of any talent for the game. But he didn't give up, earning a graduate journalism degree from Concordia University and jumping straight to a sports-writing job with the *Canadian Press*. The first time he walked into the Montréal Canadiens dressing room as a giddy cub reporter, Basu nearly fell over himself as it dawned on him that, despite his ineptitude on the ice, he had in fact been telling the truth as a dreamy-eyed eight-year-old.

Basu covers sports for the *Canadian Press* in Montréal and writes a weekly amateur sports column for the *Montréal Gazette*. He is also editor for a weekly newspaper on Montréal's South Shore, the *St-Lambert Journal*.